Jesus

WE ADORE YOU

Jesus
WE ADORE YOU
Prayers Before the Blessed Sacrament

Compiled and With an Introduction and Prayers by
Paul Thigpen

SERVANT
BOOKS

PUBLISHED BY ST. ANTHONY MESSENGER PRESS
CINCINNATI, OHIO

All Scripture quotations, unless indicated, are taken from the Revised Standard
Version of the Bible, copyrighted 1946, 1952, 1971 by the Division of Christian
Education of the National Council of Churches of Christ in the USA. Used by per-
mission.

Published by St. Anthony Messenger Press
28 W. Liberty St.
Cincinnati, OH 45202
www.servantbooks.com

Cover design by Paul Higdon, Bloomington, MN

05 06 07 08 09 10 9 8 7 6 5 4 3

Printed in the United States of America
ISBN 1-56955-235-5

Library of Congress Cataloging-in-Publication Data

Jesus, we adore you: prayers before the blessed sacrament / compiled and with an
introduction and prayers by Paul Thigpen.
    p. cm
  Includes bibliographical references.
  ISBN 1-56955-235-5 (alk. paper)
  1. Lord's Supper—Adoration—Prayer-books and devotions—English. I.
Thigpen, Thomas Paul, 1954-

  BX2045.H553 J47 2001
  242'.7—dc21

                                                              00-065917

For Rev. Joel Derks, O.S.B.,
who has taught our family so much
and who introduced us
to the treasures of Eucharistic adoration

Contents

Before the Blessed Sacrament

I adore You hiding behind this mask
this shroud of appearances wrapping the Substance
this cloud of wheat that cloaks the Sun
this veil of bread upon the Face
all creatures long to see.

I worship You waiting within this portal
this skylight open to shimmering Heavens
this doorway down to silent Depths
this darkened window dim and foggy
with the breath of Love.

For You gave Yourself to me in this Token
this Locket hung on the breast of heaven
this modest Medal of celestial mint
this poor plain Penny in the purse of God
that purchased a world.

Paul Thigpen

Introduction

"THE HIDDEN GOD"
An Invitation to Eucharistic Adoration

O happy Church! Truly, within You is a hidden God, an infinite Treasure, a plentiful redemption, an everlasting safety. Human eye cannot see, nor can any finite intelligence penetrate that ineffable, mysterious presence of heaven's great Lord, the mighty Foe to sin. O saving Host, opening wide the gate of heaven!

ST. PAUL OF THE CROSS

I felt it first as a longing, an ache that resisted all remedy, a hunger that refused to be filled. I was perplexed. What was it in these Catholic churches that wooed me whenever I visited to pray?

It was of course the Eucharistic Presence. But until I became Catholic myself and learned about that glorious, veiled Reality, I could only marvel at the peace, the joy, the strength I encountered whenever I knelt before the tabernacle. I was haunted by the Hidden God.

The day came at last when I actually tasted the Bread of heaven—could any day have been happier?—and He joined Himself to me more intimately than I could ever have imagined. But in the years since, that Feast has only sharpened the hunger for Him; as many of the saints have observed, the more we feed on Him, the more we want.

Some recent critics of Eucharistic adoration claim that devotion to the Blessed Sacrament outside Mass somehow diminishes our reception of Holy Communion within Mass. Others insist that a focus on Jesus' presence in the Eucharist somehow eclipses our view of Jesus' presence in our brothers and sisters.

Such criticisms, however, only reflect a tragic ignorance: ignorance of theology, of ecclesiology, of psychology, of history, of the lives of the saints and contemporary Eucharistic adorers of every kind. Those who make it a habit to visit Jesus in the tabernacle and in the monstrance know full well from their own transforming experience that He teaches them there to handle His Body more reverently and lovingly— whether it is His Body received in Communion or His body (in a quite different sense) the Church.

Several fine texts recently published offer an ample introduction, explanation, and defense of Eucharistic devotion: Daniel Guernsey's *Adoration: Eucharistic Texts and Prayers Throughout Church History;* Fr. John Hardon's *Catechism on the Real Presence,* and Fr. Benedict Groschel and James Monti's *In the Presence of Our Lord: The History, Theology and Psychology of Eucharistic Devotion* (see "Sources and Further Reading"). The purpose of this little volume, however, is simply to provide a prayer book for those who seek Jesus more fully and deeply in visits to the Blessed Sacrament.

Perhaps unique to this collection of Eucharistic texts is its structure, which intentionally reflects a natural progression common to devotional experience. The first chapter provides, not prayers, but rather reflections from the holy Magisterium, the saints, and other prominent Catholic sources. These are offered as an initial context to inspire a more profound meditation on the importance of Eucharistic adoration and to feed the desire to meet Jesus in this way. Such reflections, coming as they do from so diverse a range of personal, cultural, and historical settings, should also confirm for us that this particular kind of devotion is ancient, perennial, universal, and essential in the life of the Church.

How to Use This Book

Each of the chapters following offers prayers, Scriptural texts, and meditations on one particular aspect of our devotion as it unfolds before the Blessed Sacrament. First, we recognize and enter into the Lord's unique Eucharistic Presence (chapter 2). Having encountered Him there, we worship and exalt Him (chapter 3). Our experience of His holiness then naturally leads to an awareness of our own sinfulness (chapter 4), calling us to confess our sins and receive His grace to change. (Such confession, of course, is no substitute for the Sacrament of Reconciliation, but instead should complement it.)

Having asked for the grace of conversion, we're ready to listen and rest in silence before the Lord (chapter 5). What He has to say helps us shape our petitions as we bring our needs to Him (chapter 6) and pray for others as well (chapter 7). Finally, we invite the power of His Eucharistic Presence to accompany us as we go out again to serve God in the world (chapter 10).

One additional chapter provides prayers that join us to the angels and saints (chapter 8), and yet one more offers prayers for special times in the Church calendar (chapter 9).

You may find this structure useful in several ways. First, it allows you, if you wish, to choose a reading or two from each chapter in order, so that you can be led through the devotional progression described above. The advantage of this approach: It serves as a gentle reminder that prayer is not all petition but also invocation, adoration, meditation, confession, intercession, and mission. Eucharistic devotion is a banquet of many courses.

A second advantage of the structure is that it allows you to delve more deeply as needed into a particular aspect of prayer by reading through the relevant chapter. Are you exhausted just now or seeking wisdom for a difficult decision? Take up the prayers on listening and rest in Jesus' presence. Are you burdened for others you see struggling and hurting? Go to the chapter on intercession and reparation. Do you sense the need for repentance? Make your own the penitential prayers in the chapter on conversion.

Perhaps you'll discover other uses of the book as well. I found in compiling it that often a single text proved so profound that, even though at that moment I wasn't kneeling before the Blessed Sacrament, I had to lay aside everything else and dwell for a while on the words in His presence right where I was.

From Where Did These Readings Originate?

I've attributed prayers and quotations to individuals wherever possible. Nevertheless, it's the nature of prayers to tend toward anonymity as they increase in popularity: When people repeat to God another person's words because they find in them an echo of their own heart's cry, they rarely add an attribution along with their "Amen." So knowledge of sources slowly slips away as prayers are passed along. Who knows, for example, what devout believer first prayed the ancient words known as the Jesus prayer, or even the Hail Mary, for that matter? Meanwhile, we can hardly imagine the authors of such prayers frowning down on us from heaven because their names have been forgotten!

The mixed blessing of the Internet has sharpened this problem. Countless prayers and quotations appear on Catholic web sites—and I heartily welcome them there—but they often provide no clues about their provenance. Even so, I've tried to use these sparingly, choosing only the texts so meaningful that I found myself compelled to include them.

In any case, I've worked through a number of collections trying to identify sources, and if a reader can identify a source for an unattributed text, my publisher will correct the omission in future printings of the book. Most of the attributed historical texts cited are my own translations or adaptations.

In the books listed under "Sources and Further Reading," nearly all the readings in this collection will be found—except, of course, for those modest compositions born in my own heart.

These original prayers call for one last remark. Like the ancient sources, I, too, am more concerned that they be used than that they be attributed. I earnestly hope that someone will find them worth praying and share them with others to pray. The prayers are copyrighted primarily as a safeguard, to ensure that they aren't abused or misused for purposes contrary to their original intent.

Meanwhile, Jesus watches for us from the tabernacle, the monstrance, the altar. We dare not keep Him waiting. And if a skeptic, or perhaps just a curious soul, should ask us why we keep vigil there, we can recall the story once told of St. Francis of Assisi, the gentle friar who burned so fiercely with love, both for his Eucharistic Lord and for all his Lord's creatures.

When asked, "What do you do during those long hours before the Blessed Sacrament?" he answered simply: "What does the poor man do at the rich man's door, the sick man in the presence of his physician, the thirsty man at a clear stream? What they do, I do before the Eucharistic God. I pray. I adore. I love."

Paul Thigpen
October 1, 2000
Feast of St. Thérèse of Lisieux,
Adorer of Jesus in the Eucharist

ONE

"THE QUEEN OF ALL DEVOTIONS"
Meditation
Reflections on the Importance of Eucharistic Adoration

Devotion to the Blessed Sacrament is the queen of all devotions. It is the central devotion of the Church. All others gather round it, and group themselves there as satellites; for others celebrate his mysteries; this is himself. It is the universal devotion.

FR. FREDERICK WILLIAM FABER

The Catholic Church has always offered and still offers to the sacrament of the Eucharist the cult of adoration, not only during Mass but also outside of it, reserving the consecrated hosts with the utmost care, exposing them to the solemn veneration of the faithful, and carrying them in procession.

POPE PAUL VI, *MYSTERIUM FIDEI, 56*, QUOTED IN THE
CATECHISM OF THE CATHOLIC CHURCH, PAR. 1378

I am the living bread which came down from heaven; if any one eats of this bread, he will live for ever; and the bread which I shall give for the life of the world is my flesh.

JOHN 6:51

Could you not watch with Me one hour?

MATTHEW 26:40

No place is left for doubting that all Christ's faithful should in their veneration display towards this most holy Sacrament the full worship of adoration that is due to the true God, in accordance with the custom always received in the Catholic Church. For it is not the less to be adored because it was instituted by Christ the Lord that it might be taken and eaten.

THE COUNCIL OF TRENT

Tirelessly promote the cult of the Eucharist, the focus where all other forms of piety must ultimately emerge.... In the course of the day the faithful should not omit to visit the Blessed Sacrament, which according to the liturgical laws must be kept in the churches with great reverence in a most honorable location. Such visits are a proof of gratitude, and expression of love, an acknowledgment of the Lord's presence.

POPE PAUL VI

Our communal worship at Mass must go together with our personal worship of Jesus in Eucharistic adoration in order that our love may be complete.

POPE JOHN PAUL II

A more intelligent apprehension of the Blessed Sacrament will lead to a more intense love of it.

FR. FREDERICK WILLIAM FABER

I put before you the one great thing to love on earth: the Blessed Sacrament.... There you will find romance, glory, honor, fidelity, and the true way of all your loves upon earth.

J.R.R. TOLKIEN

The devotion to the Eucharist is the most noble because it has God as its object; it is the most profitable for salvation, because it gives us the Author of Grace; it is the sweetest, because the Lord is Sweetness Itself.

ST. PIUS X

I urge priests, religious and lay people to continue and redouble their efforts to teach the younger generations the meaning and value of Eucharistic adoration and devotion. How will young people be able to know the Lord If they are not introduced to the mystery of his Presence?

POPE JOHN PAUL II

There is a school in heaven, and there one has only to learn how to love. The school is in the Cenacle; the Teacher is Jesus; the matter taught is His Flesh and His Blood.

ST. GEMMA GALGANI

Let us never forget that an age prospers or dwindles in proportion to its devotion to the holy Eucharist. This is the measure of its spiritual life and its faith, of its charity and its virtue.

ST. PETER JULIAN EYMARD

My Jesus! What a lovable contrivance this holy Sacrament was—that You would hide under the appearance of bread to make Yourself loved and to be available for a visit by anyone who desires You!

ST. ALPHONSUS LIGUORI

When you look at the crucifix, you understand how much Jesus loved you then. When you look at the sacred Host, you understand how much Jesus loves you now.

MOTHER TERESA OF CALCUTTA

In this manner [Eucharistic adoration] the faithful testify to and solemnly make evident the faith of the Church according to which the Word of God and the Son of the Virgin Mary who suffered on the cross, who lies present hidden in the Eucharist, and who reigns in heaven, are believed to be identical.

POPE PIUS XII

O boundless charity! Even as You, true God and true Man, gave Yourself entirely to us, so also You left Yourself entirely for us, to be our food, so that during our earthly pilgrimage we would not faint with weariness, but would be strengthened by You, our heavenly Bread. O mercenary people! And what has your God left you? He has left you Himself, wholly God and wholly Man, concealed under the whiteness of this bread.

ST. CATHERINE OF SIENA

What wonderful majesty! What stupendous condescension! O sublime humility! That the Lord of the whole universe, God and the Son of God, should humble Himself like this under the form of a little bread, for our salvation.

ST. FRANCIS OF ASSISI

The time you spend with Jesus in the Blessed Sacrament is the best time you will spend on earth. Each moment that you spend with Jesus will deepen your union with Him and make your soul everlastingly more glorious and beautiful in heaven, and will help bring about everlasting peace on earth.

MOTHER TERESA OF CALCUTTA

"Where is the newborn King of the Jews?" inquired the three Magi of Herod, king of Jerusalem.... "We desire so much to see Him; we have made so long a journey in order to become acquainted with Him!" ... But now there is no need of traveling far or of making many inquiries to find Him. He is, as we know by faith, in our churches, not far from our homes. The Magi could find Him in one place only; we can find Him in every part of the world, wherever the Blessed Sacrament is kept. Are we then not happier than those who lived at the time of our Savior Himself?

FR. MICHAEL MULLER, C.S.S.R.

To make room in our life for the Eucharistic Lord, so that He can change our life into His—is that asking too much?

ST. TERESA BENEDICTA OF THE CROSS (EDITH STEIN)

God in His omnipotence could not give more, in His wisdom knew not how to give more, in His riches had not more to give, than the Eucharist.

ST. AUGUSTINE OF HIPPO

Every time I hear anyone speak of the Sacred Heart of Jesus or of the Blessed Sacrament I feel an indescribable joy. It is as if a wave of precious memories, sweet affections and joyful hopes swept over my poor person, making me tremble with happiness and filling my soul with tenderness. These are loving appeals from Jesus who wants me wholeheartedly there, at the source of all goodness, His Sacred Heart, throbbing mysteriously behind the Eucharistic veils.

BLESSED POPE JOHN XXIII

If we really loved the good God, we should make it our joy and happiness to come and spend a few moments to adore Him, and ask Him for the grace of forgiveness; and we should regard those moments as the happiest of our lives.

ST. JOHN VIANNEY

You may be sure that of all the moments of your life, the time you spend before the divine Sacrament will be that which will give you more strength during life and more consolation at the hour of your death and during eternity.

ST. ALPHONSUS LIGUORI

Do not say that you have no time. Rather, acknowledge that you do not love Him enough. If you did, you would leave everything in order to visit Him.

JOSÉ GUADALUPE TREVINO

I understand that, each time we contemplate with desire and devotion the Host in which is hidden Christ's Eucharistic Body, we increase our merits in heaven and secure special joys to be ours later in the beatific vision of God.

ST. GERTRUDE THE GREAT

Loving souls can find no greater delight than to be in the company of those whom they love. If we, then, love Jesus Christ much, behold we are now in His presence. Jesus in the Blessed Sacrament sees us and hears us; shall we, then, say nothing to Him? Let us console ourselves in His company; let us rejoice in His glory, and in the love which so many enamored souls bear Him in the most holy Sacrament. Let us desire that all should love Jesus in the holy Sacrament, and consecrate their hearts to Him.

ST. ALPHONSUS LIGUORI

Neither theological knowledge nor social action alone is enough to keep us in love with Christ unless both are preceded by a personal encounter with Him. Theological insights are gained not only from between two covers of a book, but from two bent knees before an altar. The holy hour becomes like an oxygen tank to revive the breath of the Holy Spirit in the midst of the foul and fetid atmosphere of the world.

ARCHBISHOP FULTON J. SHEEN

Perpetual adoration is the divine romance between Jesus and His people. It is saying "yes" to His marriage proposal. All He wants is our love.

MSGR. JOSEFINO S. RAMIREZ AND FR. MARTIN LUCIA

If souls but understood the treasure they possess in the divine Eucharist, it would be necessary to encircle the Tabernacles with the strongest ramparts for, in the delirium of a devouring and holy hunger, they would press forward themselves to feed on the Bread of Angels. The Churches would overflow with adorers consumed with love for the divine Prisoner no less by night than by day.

BLESSED DINA BELANGER

The Eucharist is the sacrament of love; it signifies love, it produces love.

ST. THOMAS AQUINAS

I beg you to show the greatest possible reverence and honor for the most holy Body and Blood of our Lord Jesus Christ, through whom all things, whether on earth or in heaven, have been brought to peace and reconciled with Almighty God.

ST. FRANCIS OF ASSISI

If the Blessed Sacrament were administered in only one place and consecrated by only one priest in the entire world, with what great a desire, do you think, would people run to that place and that priest, so that they could behold there these heavenly mysteries!

THOMAS À KEMPIS

TWO

"HIS GOODNESS WOULD HAVE YOU DRAW NEAR"
Invocation
Recognizing and Entering Jesus' Eucharistic Presence

Invocation is as follows: Having placed your soul in the presence of God, you must humble it with deep reverence, acknowledging yourself unworthy to approach His Sovereign Majesty, yet knowing that His goodness would have you draw near, and therefore asking of Him grace to serve and worship Him in your meditation.

ST. FRANCES DE SALES

Begin all prayer ... by placing yourself in the presence of God.... We should always, before we pray, excite our souls to an attentive recollection of the presence of God.

ST. FRANCES DE SALES

Jesus said to them, "I am the Bread of life; he who comes to me shall not hunger, and he who believes in me shall never thirst."

JOHN 6:35

O my Jesus, dwelling in the Blessed Sacrament, as the humblest of Your creatures, lost in my own nothingness, prostrate before the throne of Your great Majesty, profoundly I adore You with all my spirit, with all the powers of my soul. Here I acknowledge You, veiled beneath the sacramental species, as my God, my Creator, my last end.

With true and living faith I believe that in this adorable Sacrament, You Yourself, true God and true Man, are present; You who, being the only-begotten Son of God, yet because of Your great love for man, took to Yourself human flesh in the most pure womb of Mary ever-virgin, by the operation of the Holy Spirit. Therefore You were born poor, in a lowly manger; therefore You lived subject to men.

Now that, having conquered death and hell, You sit glorious at the right hand of Your Father, I believe that, without abandoning the heavenly throne of Your glory, You nevertheless dwell substantially and really in this ineffable Sacrament, in which I glorify You as God in the firmament of Your Church, as the Lamb enthroned upon His seat of love, as the Priest of the sanctuary of all grace, as the sweet Manna of all consolation, and as the Arbiter of my eternal fate in this court of mercy. Yes, my dear Jesus, all this I declare and believe, as You have commanded me, and as Your spouse, the Catholic Church, my mother, teaches. Amen.

St. Philip Neri

My Lord Jesus Christ, for the love You bear mankind, You remain night and day in this Sacrament, full of compassion and love, waiting, calling, welcoming all who come to visit You. I believe that You are present in the Sacrament of the altar. I adore You from the depths of my own nothingness. I thank You for the many graces You have given me, and especially for having given me Yourself in this Sacrament.

St. Alphonsus Liguori

When we remain in silence before the Blessed Sacrament, it is Christ totally and really present whom we discover, whom we adore, and with whom we are in contact.

Pope John Paul II

God Himself is with us:
Let us now adore Him
And with awe appear before Him.
God is in His temple:
All within keep silence
And before Him bow with reverence.

Him alone
God we own;
To our Lord and Savior
Praises sing forever!

Gerhard Teerstegen

I will not leave you desolate; I will come to you. Yet a little while, and the world will see me no more, but you will see me; because I live, you will live also.

JOHN 14:18-19

Hail, true Body, truly born
of the Virgin Mary mild;
truly offered, wracked and torn,
on the cross for all defiled;
from whose love-pierced, sacred side
flowed Thy true Blood's saving tide:
Be a foretaste sweet to me
in my death's great agony,
O my loving, Gentle One,
sweetest Jesus, Mary's Son. Amen.

ATTRIBUTED TO POPE INNOCENT IV

God is as really present in the consecrated Host as He is in the glory of heaven.

ST. PASCHAL BABYLON

O King of glory, though You hide Your beauty, yet the eye of my soul rends the veil. I see the angelic choirs giving You honor without cease.

ST. FAUSTINA KOWALSKA

When He was at table with them, He took the bread and blessed, and broke it, and gave it to them. And their eyes were open and they recognized Him.

LUKE 24:30-31

I keep the Lord always before me; because He is at my right hand, I shall not be moved. Therefore my heart is glad, and my soul rejoices; my body also dwells secure.... Thou dost show me the path of life; in thy presence there is fulness of joy, in thy right hand are pleasures for evermore.

PSALM 16:8-9, 11

O blessed Host, enchantment of all heaven, though Your beauty be veiled and captured in a crumb of bread, strong faith tears away that veil.

ST. FAUSTINA KOWALSKA

Serve the Lord with gladness! Come into His presence with singing! Know that the Lord is God! It is He that made us, and we are His; we are His people, and the sheep of His pasture.

PSALM 100:2-3

I acknowledge and confess that I kneel before that sacred Humanity, which was conceived in Mary's womb, and lay in Mary's bosom; which grew up to man's estate, and by the Sea of Galilee called the Twelve, wrought miracles, and spoke words of wisdom and peace; which in due season hung on the cross, lay in the tomb, rose from the dead, and now reigns in heaven. I praise, bless, and give myself wholly to Him, who is the true Bread of my soul, and my everlasting joy.

VENERABLE JOHN HENRY NEWMAN

God is everywhere, in the very air I breathe, yes everywhere, but in His Sacrament of the altar He is as present actually and really as my soul within my body; in His Sacrifice daily offered as really as once offered on the cross.

ST. ELIZABETH ANN SETON

The God of the Eucharist conceals Himself in order to be desired, veils Himself in order to become an object of contemplation; He wraps Himself in mystery in order to spur on and perfect the soul's love.

ST. PETER JULIAN EYMARD

Do you realize that Jesus is there in the tabernacle expressly for you—for you alone? He burns with the desire to come into your heart.

ST. THÉRÈSE OF LISIEUX

That eternal Spring is hidden
yet I know well where it flows....
I know that there can be
nothing else so beautiful
and that the heavens and the earth drink there....
I know well that its bottom cannot be found
and that no one can penetrate its depths....
Its clarity is never muddied,
and I know that every light has come from it....
Well do I know how vast, how mighty is the flow
of the stream born in this Fount....
This eternal Spring is hidden
in this living Bread to give us life....
It is here calling to creatures
and from its water they quench their thirst....
This living Fount that I long for
I see in this Bread of Life....

ST. JOHN OF THE CROSS

Let others seek instead of You whatever they will, but nothing pleases me or will please me but You, my God, my Hope, my everlasting Salvation. I will not be silent, I will not cease praying until Your grace returns to me and You speak inwardly to me, saying: "Behold, I am here. Lo, I have come to you because you have called Me. Your tears and the desire of your soul, your humility and contrition of heart have inclined Me and brought Me to you."

THOMAS À KEMPIS

Then I said, "Lo, I have come to do thy will, O God."

HEBREWS 10:7

I throw myself at the foot of the tabernacle like a dog at the foot of his Master.

ST. JOHN VIANNEY

One thing have I asked of the Lord, that will I seek after;
that I may dwell in the house of the Lord
all the days of my life,
to behold the beauty of the Lord,
and to inquire in his temple.

PSALM 27:4

O little key! I envy you,
for you can open, at any hour,
the Eucharistic prison house,
where the God of love and might dwells.
And yet—O tender mystery!—
one effort of my faith alone
unlocks the tabernacle door,
and hides me there with Christ.

ST. THÉRÈSE OF LISIEUX

Here, in the Sacrament of the altar, You are wholly present, my Lord God, my Lord the God-Man Christ Jesus; here we freely partake of the fruit of eternal salvation ... not through levity, curiosity, or sentimentality, but only firm faith, devout hope, and sincere love. O God, invisible Creator of the world, how marvelous are Your dealings with us! How sweetly and graciously You welcome Your chosen, to whom You offer Yourself in this glorious Sacrament! It truly passes all understanding, it kindles the love and draws the hearts of all the faithful to Yourself.

THOMAS À KEMPIS

It is not to remain in a golden monstrance that He comes down each day from heaven, but to find another heaven, the heaven of our soul, in which He takes delight.

ST. THÉRÈSE OF LISIEUX

Let all mortal flesh keep silence
and with fear and trembling stand;
ponder nothing earthly-minded,
for with blessing in His hand
Christ our God to earth descends,
our full homage to demand.

King of Kings yet born of Mary
as of old on earth He stood;
Lord of Lords in human vesture
in the Body and the Blood.
He will give to all the faithful
His own self for heavenly food.

FROM THE LITURGY OF ST. JAMES

O Jesus, present in the Blessed Sacrament in our churches, You give us solace and refuge; You give us faith, hope, love, and hospitality. You build for us an inner retreat, an ardent repose. Help us to seek You and find You.

VENERABLE CHARLES DE FOUCAULD

There, hidden beneath the white appearances of the sacred Host, Jesus is truly and personally present.... What more shall we possess in heaven? The manner of the possession will be different, but its object is essentially the same. The Eucharist is the essence of heaven on earth.

JOSÉ GUADALUPE TREVINO

The presence of Jesus in the Eucharist is proof that His love for us has no sunset.... In the Holy Eucharist the only Son of God, Jesus Christ, fulfills His promise to be with us always.

MSGR. JOHN MOLONEY, P.P.

O wonderful loftiness and stupendous dignity!
O sublime humility! O humble sublimity!
The Lord of the universe, God and the Son of God,
so humbles Himself that He hides Himself
for our salvation
under an ordinary piece of bread!
See the humility of God, brothers, and pour out
your hearts before Him!
Humble yourselves so that you may be exalted by Him!
Hold back nothing of yourselves for yourselves,
so that He who gives Himself totally to you
may receive you totally!

ST. FRANCIS OF ASSISI

I am just a speck of dust,
but I want to make my dwelling
in the shadow of the sanctuary
with the Prisoner of Love.
Ah! my soul longs for the Host.
I love Him and want nothing more.
It is the hidden God who attracts me.
I am the atom of Jesus.

ST. THÉRÈSE OF LISIEUX

O Jesus, here present in the holy Eucharist, Your heart is all aglow with love for me! You call me, You urge me to come to You—even more: You descend from Your throne, You leave Your Tabernacle, to enter my poor heart.

You crave to dwell in my heart. Ah, that I could prepare for You a fitting abode! Send forth the fire of Your love, and in Your mercy make my cold, lukewarm heart burn for You! Amen.

ST. ILDEPHONSUS

At the feet of Jesus in the Blessed Sacrament, let your hearts through the grace of God and the sacrifices you perform be like a golden thurible. Your generous hearts will be as it were incandescent pieces of charcoal. Your purity will become incense which, as it is consumed, gives joy to the Heart of Jesus through the perfume rising from it.

MARIE-DELUIL MARTINY, MOTHER MARY OF JESUS

O Jesus, You instituted this Sacrament, not through any desire to draw some advantage from it for Yourself, but solely moved by love that has no other measure than to be without measure. You instituted this Sacrament because Your love exceeds all words. Burning with love for us, You desired to give Yourself to us and took up Your dwelling in the consecrated Host, entirely and forever, until the end of time. And You did this, not only to give us a memorial of Your death that is our salvation, but You did it also, to remain with us entirely and forever.

ST. ANGELA OF FOLIGNO

In the presence of Jesus in the holy Sacrament we ought to be like the blessed ones in heaven before the Divine Essence.

ST. TERESA OF AVILA

THREE

"ALL MY HEART SHOULD BURN AND WEEP FOR JOY"
Adoration
Worshipping Jesus in the Blessed Sacrament

> O Lord Jesus, ... all my heart should burn and weep
> for joy to see You and Your holy angels, for I truly
> have You present with me, though You are hidden
> under other appearances.
>
> THOMAS À KEMPIS

I adore You, Jesus, true God and true Man, present in the holy Eucharist, kneeling before You and united in spirit with all the faithful on earth and all the saints in heaven. In gratitude for so great a blessing, I love You with all my heart, for You are worthy of all praise and adoration.

Lord Jesus Christ, may I never offend You with my lack of love. May Your Eucharistic Presence refresh me in body and soul. Mary, Mother of the Eucharistic Lord, pray for me and obtain for me a greater love for Jesus. Amen.

O Sacred Banquet, in which Christ is received, the memory of his Passion is renewed, the mind is filled with grace, and a

pledge of future glory given to us.
Thou didst give them Bread from heaven;
Containing in itself all sweetness.
Let us pray: O God, who under a wonderful Sacrament hast
left us a memorial of Thy passion; grant us, we beseech
Thee, so to reverence the sacred mysteries of Thy Body and
Blood, that we may ever feel within ourselves the fruit of Thy
redemption: who livest and reignest for ever and ever. Amen.

O Sacrament most holy, O Sacrament divine,
all praise and all thanksgiving be every moment Thine!

O Lord Jesus,... my eyes couldn't bear to behold You in Your
own divine brilliance, nor could all the world bear to behold
You in the light and glory of Your majesty. Thus You greatly
help me in my weakness by hiding Yourself under this holy
Sacrament.

I truly possess and worship the One whom the angels worship in heaven—but I worship Him only by faith, while they
worship with a clear vision of Him in His own unhidden
Likeness. So, then, I must be content with the light of true
faith, and to walk in it until the day of everlasting Light will
appear and the shadow of images will pass away.

THOMAS À KEMPIS

O come, let us worship and bow down,
let us kneel before the Lord, our Maker!
for He is our God,
and we are the people of His pasture,
and the sheep of His hand.

PSALM 95:6-7

May the heart of Jesus in the Most Blessed Sacrament be praised, adored, and loved with grateful affection at every moment in all the tabernacles of the world, now and until the end of time!

Jesus veiled! Let us kneel down before Him in adoring awe, while our Mother teaches us His beauty, and His sweetness, and His goodness, and His nearness. When we think we know Him we shall not know the half, and when we speak of Him we shall stammer as children do, and when our hearts are hot with love of Him, they will be cold in comparison of the love which is His due.

FR. FREDERICK WILLIAM FABER

For who is Lord but our Lord? Or who is God besides our God? Most high, most excellent, most mighty, most omnipotent; most merciful and most just; most hidden and most near; most beautiful and most strong; constant, yet incomprehensible;

unchangeable, yet changing all things; never new, never old; renewing all things, yet bringing old age upon the proud, without their knowing it; always working, yet always at rest; gathering, yet needing nothing; upholding, filling, and protecting; creating, nourishing, and perfecting; still seeking, though You lack nothing.

St. Augustine of Hippo

To the King of ages, immortal, invisible, the only God, be honor and glory for ever and ever. Amen.

1 Timothy 1:17

Hidden God, devoutly I adore Thee, truly present
  underneath these veils:
All my heart subdues itself before Thee, since it all
  before Thee faints and fails.
Not to sight, or taste, or touch be credit; hearing only
  do we trust secure;
I believe, for God the Son has said it—Word of truth
  that ever shall endure.

On the cross was veiled Thy Godhead's splendor, here
  Thy manhood lies hidden too;
unto both alike my faith I render and, as sued
  the contrite thief, I sue.
Though I look not on Thy wounds with Thomas,
  Thee, my Lord, and Thee, my God, I call:

Make me more and more believe Thy promise,
    hope in Thee, and love Thee over all.
O memorial of my Savior, dying, living Bread
    that gives life to man;
make my soul, its life from Thee supplying,
    taste Thy sweetness, as on earth it can.
Contemplating, Lord, Thy hidden presence,
    grant me what I thirst for and implore,
in the revelation of Thy essence to behold
    Thy glory evermore. Amen.

St. Thomas Aquinas

We adore You, most holy Lord Jesus Christ, here in all Your churches throughout the whole world, because by Your holy cross, You have redeemed the world.

St. Francis of Assisi

    Praise the Lord!
    Praise, O servants of the Lord,
    praise the name of the Lord!
    Blessed be the name of the Lord
    from this time forth and for evermore!
    From the rising of the sun to its setting
    the name of the Lord is to be praised!

Psalm 113:1-3

I adore You, Lord and Creator, hidden in the Most Blessed Sacrament. I adore You for all the works of Your hands, that reveal to me so much wisdom, goodness, and mercy, O Lord. You have spread so much beauty over the earth, and it tells me about Your beauty, even though these beautiful things are but a faint reflection of You, incomprehensible Beauty. And although You have hidden Yourself and concealed Your beauty, my eye, enlightened by faith, reaches You and my soul recognizes its Creator, its highest Good, and my heart is completely immersed in prayer of adoration.

ST. FAUSTINA KOWALSKA

To the only God, our Savior through Jesus Christ our Lord, be glory, majesty, dominion, and authority, before all time and now and for ever! Amen.

JUDE 25

I believe that You, O Jesus, are in the most holy Sacrament. I love You and desire You. Come into my heart. I embrace You. Never leave me. May the burning and most sweet power of Your love, O Lord Jesus Christ, I beseech You, absorb my mind that I may die through love of Your love, who were graciously pleased to die through love of my love.

ST. FRANCIS OF ASSISI

O marvelous Sacrament! How can I find words to praise You! You are the Life of the soul, the Medicine healing our wounds, our Comforter when we are overburdened, the memorial of Jesus Christ, the Proof of His love, the most precious Precept of His testament, our Companion in the pilgrimage of life, the Joy sustaining us in our exile, the burning Coal kindling the fire of divine love, the Instrument of grace, the Pledge of eternal bliss and the Treasure of Christians.

LOUIS OF GRANADA

O Jesus of the Eucharist! O consecrated host! O envied mostrance! O blessed ciborium, beloved of my heart! The tabernacle is my treasure, and, far or near, my eyes never lose sight of it, for it contains the God of Love.

SERVANT OF GOD CONCEPCIÓN CABRERA DE ARMIDA

Jesus, my Lord, my God, my All,
how can I love Thee as I ought?
And how revere this wondrous gift,
so far surpassing hope or thought?

Had I but Mary's sinless heart,
to love Thee with, my dearest King
O! with what bursts of fervent praise,
Thy goodness, Jesus, would I sing!

Ah, see! Within a creature's hand
the vast Creator deigns to be,
Reposing, infant-like, as though
on Joseph's arm, or Mary's knee.

Thy Body, Soul, and Godhead, all;
O mystery of love divine!
I cannot compass all I have,
for all Thou hast and art are mine.

 Sound, sound His praises higher still,
and come, ye angels, to our aid;
'Tis God, 'tis God, the very God,
whose power both man and angels made.
Sweet Sacrament, we Thee adore!
O make us love Thee more and more!

FR. FREDRICK WILLIAM FABER

Most Holy Trinity, I adore Thee! My God, my God,
I love Thee in the Most Blessed Sacrament!

EUCHARISTIC PRAYER OF FATIMA

Now, my tongue, the mystery telling,
of the glorious Body sing,
and the Blood, all price excelling,
which the gentiles' Lord and King,
in a Virgin's womb once dwelling,
shed for this world's ransoming.

Given for us, and condescending,
to be born for us below,
He, with men in converse blending,
dwelt the seed of truth to sow,
till He closed with wondrous ending
His most patient life of woe.

That last night, at supper lying,
'mid the Twelve, His chosen band,
Jesus, with the law complying,
keeps the feast its rites demand;
then, more precious food supplying,
gives Himself with His own hand.

Word-made-flesh true bread He maketh
by His word His Flesh to be;
wine His Blood; which whoso taketh
must from carnal thoughts be free;
faith alone, though sight forsaketh,
shows true hearts the mystery.

Therefore we, before Him bending,
this great Sacrament revere;
types and shadows have their ending,
for the newer rite is here;
faith, our outward sense befriending,
makes our inward vision clear.

Glory let us give, and blessing
to the Father, and the Son,
honor, might, and praise addressing,

> while eternal ages run;
> ever too His love confessing,
> who from both with both is one.

St. Thomas Aquinas

Let every knee bend before Thee, O greatness of my God, so supremely humbled in the sacred Host. May every heart love Thee, every spirit adore Thee, and every will be subject to Thee!

St. Margaret Mary Alacoque

O You who are hidden, Body, Soul, and Divinity, under the fragile form of bread, You are my life from whom springs an abundance of graces; and, for me, You surpass the delights of heaven.

St. Faustina Kowalska

When you awake in the night, transport yourself quickly in spirit before the Tabernacle, saying: "Behold, my God, I come to adore You, to praise, thank, and love You, and to keep You company with all the angels."

St. John Vianney

Alleluia! Bread of heaven, here on earth our food and stay!
Alleluia! here the sinful flee to Thee from day to day.
Intercessor, Friend of sinners, earth's Redeemer,
    plead for me.
Where the songs of all the sinless sweep across
    the crystal sea.

Alleluia! King eternal, Thee the Lord of lords we own;
Alleluia! born of Mary, earth Thy footstool,
　　heaven Thy throne.
Thou within the veil hast entered, robed in flesh,
　　our great High Priest.
Thou on earth both Priest and Victim in the Eucharistic Feast.

WILLIAM CHATTERDON DIX

Let weak and frail man come here in humble entreaty to
adore the Sacrament of Christ, not to discuss high things, or
to wish to penetrate difficulties, but to bow down to secret
things in humble veneration, and to abandon God's mysteries to God, for Truth deceives no man—Almighty God can
do all things.

ST. PAUL OF THE CROSS

Remember, O my Jesus....
Remember that in ascending to God,
You would not leave us orphans,
But making Yourself a Prisoner on earth among us,
You veiled all Your glory....
The shadow of Your veil is pure and bright,
You living Bread of faith, Food of heaven,
O mystery of love!
You are my daily Bread, Jesus....
Remember that, in spite of all the blasphemies hurled
against this Sacrament of love,

You want to show how much You love me
by fixing Your dwelling place in a heart like mine.
O Bread of exiled souls! Holy, divine Host!
No more is it I who live; I live in You.
I am Your chosen ciborium.
Come, Jesus, come!
You are my Love.

St. Thérèse of Lisieux

O God of love, my Savior, eternally sweet and tender, heart and soul I thirst for You! You fill my soul; and yet the more I taste of You, the more I hunger. The deeper I drink of You, the more I thirst. Come, Jesus! Come, Lord!

St. Gertrude the Great

Act of Adoration
of Jesus in the Blessed Sacrament

Jesus, my God, I adore You, here present in the Blessed Sacrament of the altar, where You wait day and night to be our comfort while we await Your unveiled presence in heaven.

Jesus, my God, I adore You in all places where the Blessed Sacrament is reserved and where sins are committed against this Sacrament of love.

Jesus, my God, I adore You for all time, past, present and future, for every soul that ever was, is, or shall be created.

Jesus, my God, who for us has endured hunger and cold, labor and fatigue, I adore You.

Jesus, my God, who for my sake has deigned to subject Yourself to the humiliation of temptation, to the perfidy and defection of friends, to the scorn of Your enemies, I adore You.

Jesus, my God, who for us has endured the buffeting of Your passion, the scourging, the crowning with thorns, the heavy weight of the cross, I adore You.

Jesus, my God, who, for my salvation and that of all mankind, was cruelly nailed to the cross and hung there for three long hours in bitter agony, I adore You.

Jesus, my God, who for love of us instituted this Blessed Sacrament and offered Yourself daily for the sins of men, I adore You.

Jesus, my God, who in Holy Communion became the food of my soul, I adore You.

Jesus, for You I live. Jesus, for You I die. Jesus, I am Yours in life and death. Amen.

The Divine Praises

Blessed be God.

Blessed be His holy Name.

Blessed be Jesus Christ, true God and true man.

Blessed be the name of Jesus.

Blessed be His Most Sacred Heart.

Blessed be Jesus in the most holy Sacrament of the altar.

Blessed be the Holy Spirit, the Paraclete.

Blessed be the great Mother of God, Mary most holy.

Blessed be her holy and immaculate conception.

Blessed be her glorious assumption.

Blessed be the name of Mary, Virgin and Mother.

Blessed be St. Joseph, her most chaste spouse.

Blessed be God in His angels and in His saints.

May the heart of Jesus, in the Most Blessed Sacrament, be praised, adored, and loved with grateful affection, at every moment, in all the tabernacles of the world, even to the end of time. Amen.

Let us adore forever the most holy Sacrament.

O praise the Lord, all you nations;

Praise Him, all you people.

For His mercy is confirmed upon us;

and the truth of the Lord remains forever.

Glory be to the Father, and to the Son,

and to the Holy Spirit.

as it was in the beginning, is now, and ever shall be,

world without end. Amen.

Let us adore forever the most holy Sacrament.

FOUR

"CREATE IN ME A CLEAN HEART"
Conversion
Becoming Like Jesus

Create in me a clean heart, O God, and put a new and right spirit within me.
Cast me not away from Thy presence, and take not Thy Holy Spirit from me.

PSALM 51:10-11

Jesus said to them, "I am the bread of life; he who comes to Me shall not hunger, and he who believes in Me shall never thirst.... All that the Father gives Me will come to me; and him who comes to Me I will not cast out."

JOHN 6:35, 37

Lord Jesus Christ, Son of God,
have mercy on me, a sinner.

Have mercy on me, O God, according to thy steadfast love;
according to thy abundant mercy blot out my transgressions.
Wash me thoroughly from my iniquity,
and cleanse me from my sin!
For I know my transgressions,
and my sin is ever before me.
Against thee, thee only, have I sinned,
and done that which is evil in thy sight,
so that thou art justified in thy sentence
and blameless in thy judgment.
Behold, I was brought forth in iniquity,
and in sin did my mother conceive me.
Behold, Thou desirest truth in the inward being;
therefore teach me wisdom in my secret heart....
Wash me, and I shall be whiter than snow.
Fill me with joy and gladness;
let the bones which Thou hast broken rejoice.
Hide Thy face from my sins,
and blot out all my iniquities....
Restore to me the joy of Thy salvation,
and uphold me with a willing spirit....
The sacrifice acceptable to God is a broken spirit;
a broken and contrite heart,
O God, Thou wilt not despise.

PSALM 51:1-9, 12-17

Confession Before the Blessed Sacrament

Grain of God,
I was the stone that ground You.
Holocaust of heaven,
I was the flame that consumed You.
Lamb on the altar,
I was the knife across Your throat.
Crucified One,
I was the nail in Your hand.

Have mercy, Jesus.
Reshape this guilty soul to make
a stone in Your altar,
a flame in Your lamp,
a knife for Your Bread,
a nail in Your table
where the world sits down
to feast.

PAUL THIGPEN

Repent therefore, and turn again, that your sins may be blotted out, that times of refreshing may come from the presence of the Lord.

ACTS 3:19

What tortuous ways I walked! Woe to that rash soul of mine, which hoped by abandoning You, Lord, to find something better! It tossed and turned, upon its back, upon its sides, upon its belly, yet it found every place it lay to be hard—You alone are my rest. And behold, You are near at hand, and You deliver us from our wretched wanderings, and You settle us in Your own way. And You comfort us, saying: "Run, I will carry you; yes, I will lead you to the end of your journey, and there also I will carry you."

ST. AUGUSTINE OF HIPPO

I look and look, and turn to look again at the consecrated Host; its whiteness dazzles me; its brilliant rays wound my soul to its utmost depths by revealing to me all its defects and deformities.... Who can think himself humble in the presence of Him who is hidden under the form of bread?...

Oh, my Lord! In your presence, I ought to feel nought but shame, and a deep sense of my utter worthlessness; but I also feel a great love for You ... which purifies and transforms me, and takes me far away from this earth, to the purest of Hosts, the very abode of Love.

SERVANT OF GOD CONCEPCIÓN CABRERA DE ARMIDA

The Blessed Sacrament is the magnet of souls. There is a mutual attraction between Jesus and the souls of men. Mary drew Him down from heaven. Our nature attracted Him rather than the nature of angels. Our misery caused Him to stoop to our lowness. Even our sins had a sort of attraction for the abundance of His mercy and the predilection of His grace. Our repentance wins Him to us. Our love makes earth a paradise to Him; and our souls lure Him as gold lures the miser, with irresistible fascination.

FR. FREDERICK WILLIAM FABER

Eternal Father, I offer You the Sacred Heart of Jesus here in the Eucharist, with all its love, all its sufferings and all its merits: to expiate all the sins I have committed this day, and during all my life; to purify the good I have done in my poor way this day, and during all my life; to make up for the good I ought to have done and that I have neglected this day and during all my life. Amen.

Good Lord, forgive me those sins which through my own fault, through evil inclinations and evil habits, I cannot recognize as sin because my reason has become so blinded by sensuality. And illumine, good Lord, my heart, and give me Your grace to know these sins and to acknowledge them; and forgive me the sins I have forgotten through negligence, and bring them to my mind with grace so that I might confess them rightly.

ST. THOMAS MORE

O amiable Jesus, who has given us, in the adorable Eucharist, so convincing a proof of Your infinite love, permit us to thank You, in the name of all Your creatures, for the many blessings contained in this one precious Gift. We adore You, O hidden Deity, and most fervently wish we could offer You such love as would atone for our own offenses and for those committed by all mankind against this most adorable Mystery of love.

We ask pardon, O Lord, for the transgressions we have committed against You. We are truly sorry for having offended You, because You are infinitely good. A contrite and humble heart You will not despise. We desire to love You more and more, and we beg You for the grace of perseverance.

THE BLESSED SACRAMENT: GOD WITH US

Too late have I come to love You, Beauty so ancient, so new! Yes, too late have I come to love You! You were within me, yet I was looking for You outside myself. I, in my ugliness, rushed headlong into the things of beauty You had made. You were with me, but I was not with You. The things You had created kept me far from You; yet if they had not been in You, they would not have been at all.

You called to me and cried aloud, and You broke through my deafness. You flashed, and shone, and chased away my blindness. You breathed upon me fragrantly; I drew in my breath, and now I pant for You. I tasted, and now I hunger and thirst for You. You touched me, and I burned to enjoy Your peace.

ST. AUGUSTINE OF HIPPO

There has never yet been a bomb invented that is half so powerful as one mortal sin—and yet there is no positive power in sin, only negation, only annihilation: and perhaps that is why it is so destructive, it is a nothingness, and where it is, there is nothing left—a blank, a moral vacuum.

THOMAS MERTON

Even though You, Lord, are the same forever and ever, You do not remain angry with us forever. For You take pity on us, who are only dust and ashes. It was pleasing in Your sight to transform what was deformed in me; and by inward stings You disturbed me, so that I would be dissatisfied until I could see You clearly with the eye of my soul. By the secret hand of Your healing my swelling was relieved; and the disordered and darkened eye of my mind was day by day made whole by the stinging salve of a healthy sorrow.

ST. AUGUSTINE OF HIPPO

Poor, pitiable sinners, do not turn away from Me.... Day and night I am on the watch for you in the tabernacle. I will not reproach you.... I will not cast your sins in your face.... But I will wash them in My blood and in My wounds. No need to be afraid.... Come to Me.... If you but knew how dearly I love you.

JESUS TO SR. JOSEFA MENENDEZ

> The things, good Lord, that I pray for,
> give me the grace to labor for.
>
> ST. THOMAS MORE

I was a poor fool, seething like the sea. Forsaking You, Lord, I followed the violent course of my own torrents. I rushed past all Your lawful bounds, and I did not escape Your scourges. For what mortal can escape them? But You were always beside me, mercifully angry, ruining all my illicit pleasures with bitter discontent—all to draw me on so that I might instead seek pleasures that were free from discontent. But where could I find such pleasures except in You, Lord? I could find them only in You, who teach us by sorrow, and wound us in order to heal us, and kill us so that we may not die apart from You.

ST. AUGUSTINE OF HIPPO

O Mystery worthy of the admiration of angels! Mystery, whose excellence is infinitely enhanced by the end which the King of glory proposes to Himself in reducing Himself to so abject a condition! This truly hidden God has withdrawn into the obscurity of His tabernacle to console the afflicted, sustain the tempted, enrich the impoverished, protect the unfortunate, heal the sick, and load with benefits all those who visit Him.

My God, we believe in this excess of love, and yet we languish in a degrading lukewarmness. We requite such matchless tenderness with the darkest ingratitude. Culpable that we are, we know, O great God, that You are present on the altar, and yet we sin in every possible way against the respect that is due You. The angels tremble in Your presence; the princes of the heavenly court humble themselves into the abyss of their nothingness. It is we alone, vile vermin that we are, who dare to appear before Your tremendous Majesty in an irreverent posture. You invite us to Your adorable Banquet, but we are desirous only of perishable food, while we receive without desire the Bread of Angels.

O divine Son, veiled under the sacramental species! Melt, I beg You, this icy heart of mine, and inflame it with the sacred fire of Your love, so that it may be a fiery furnace before Your Tabernacle from which the incense of devotion may perpetually ascend to You. Amen.

FRANÇOIS FENELON

Acts of Contrition

O my God, I am heartily sorry for having offended You. I detest all my sins because of Your just punishments, but most of all because they offend You, my God, who are all-good and deserving of all my love. I firmly resolve, with the help of Your grace, to sin no more and to avoid the near occasion of sin. Amen.

My God, I am sorry for my sins with all my heart. In choosing to do wrong and failing to do good, I have sinned against You whom I should love above all things. I firmly intend, with Your help, to do penance, to sin no more, and to avoid whatever leads me to sin. Our Savior Jesus Christ suffered and died for us. In His name, my God, have mercy. Amen.

O Lord Jesus, Lover of our souls, who, for the great love with which You loved us, willed not the death of a sinner, but rather that he should be converted and live, I grieve from the bottom of my heart that I have offended You, my most loving Father and Redeemer, to whom all sin is infinitely displeasing, who so loved me that You shed Your blood for me, and endured the bitter torments of a most cruel death. O my God, my infinite Goodness, would that I never offended You. Pardon me, O Lord Jesus, as I most humbly implore Your mercy. Have pity on a sinner for whom Your blood pleads before the face of the Father.

O merciful and forgiving Lord, for the love of You, I forgive all who have ever offended me. I firmly resolve to forsake and flee from all sins, and to avoid the occasions of them, to confess, in bitterness of spirit, all those sins which I committed against Your divine goodness, and to love You, O my God, for Your own sake, above all things and forever. Grant me grace so to do, most gracious Lord Jesus. Amen.

Act of Faith

O my God, I firmly believe that You are one God in three divine Persons, Father, Son, and Holy Spirit. I believe that Your divine Son became Man and died for our sins, and that He will come to judge the living and the dead. I believe these and all the truths which the Holy Catholic Church teaches, because in revealing them You can neither deceive nor be deceived.

Act of Hope

O my God, relying on Your almighty power and infinite mercy and promises, I hope to obtain pardon of my sins, the help of Your grace and life everlasting, through the merits of Jesus Christ, my Lord and Redeemer. Amen.

Act of Charity

O my God, I love You above all things with my whole heart and soul because You are all good and worthy of all my love. I love my neighbor as myself for the love of You. I forgive all who have injured me and ask pardon of all whom I have injured. Amen.

Act of Humility

O divine Lord, how shall I dare to approach You, I who have so often offended You? No, Lord, I am not worthy that You should enter under my roof; but speak only the word and my soul shall be healed.

Act of Consecration

Lord Jesus Christ, I consecrate myself today anew and without reserve to Your divine Heart. I consecrate to You my body with all its senses, my soul with all its faculties, my entire being. I consecrate to You all my thoughts, words, and deeds, all my sufferings and labors, all my hopes, consolations, and joys. In particular I consecrate to You this poor heart of mine so that it may love only You and may be consumed as a victim in the fire of Your love.

I place my trust in You without reserve, and I hope for the remission of my sins through Your infinite mercy. I place within Your hands all my cares and anxieties. I promise to love You and to honor You till the last moment of my life, and to spread, as much as I can, devotion to Your most Sacred Heart.

Do with me what You will, my Jesus. I deserve no other reward except Your greater glory and Your holy love. Take this offering of myself and give me a place within Your divine Heart forever. Amen.

FIVE

"THE SECRET WHISPERINGS OF JESUS"
Silence
Listening and Resting in His Eucharistic Presence

Blessed is the soul who hears the Lord speaking within, who receives the word of consolation from His lips. Blessed are the ears that catch the secret whisperings of Jesus, and pay no heed to the murmurings of this world.

THOMAS À KEMPIS

This is my beloved Son, with whom I am well pleased; listen to him.

MATTHEW 17:5

Hail, sacred tabernacles!... O, I love Your temple! It is an island of peace in the ocean of the world.... Is there a tongue equal to the ecstasy of the heart? Whatever my lips may say, this blood that circulates in me, this breast that breathes in You, this heart that beats and swells, these tear-bathed eyes, this still silence—all of these pray within me. Just as the waves swell at the rising of the King of day, the stars revolve, mute with reverence and love, and You understand their silent hymn, so, Lord, in the same way, understand me; hear what I say without speaking. Silence is the highest voice of a heart that is overcome with Your glory!

St. Paul of the Cross

If you wish Me to take My rest in you, prepare for My coming by acts of self-denial.... Master your imagination and calm the tumult of your passions.... Then in the stillness of your soul you will hear My voice speaking gently within you: Today you are My repose, but for all eternity I shall be your rest.

Jesus to Sr. Josefa Menendez

Blessed indeed are the ears that listen, not to the voice of outward speech, but to the truth that teaches within the soul.

Blessed are the eyes that are closed to exterior things and are fixed upon those which are interior.

Blessed are they who penetrate inwardly, who try daily to prepare themselves more and more to understand mysteries.

Blessed are they who long to give their time to God, and who cut themselves off from the hindrances of the world.

Consider these things, my soul, and close the door of your senses, so that you can hear what the Lord your God speaks within you. "I am your salvation," says your Beloved. "I am your peace and your life. Remain with Me and you will find peace. Dismiss all passing things and seek the eternal."

Thomas à Kempis

Your Scripture is like a deep forest, and there are those who, like deer, have withdrawn there to be refreshed, where they roam, and walk, and feed, and lie down to chew on what they have found. Perfect me, Lord, and reveal their secrets to me. See how Your voice is my joy; Your voice surpasses all the abundance of my pleasures.

Give me the wisdom that I love, for I do love it, and this love of wisdom is itself a gift from You. Do not abandon Your gifts, or despise the grass that thirsts for You. Let me confess to You everything I find in Your Book, and let me hear the voice of Your praise. Let me drink You in and consider the wonderful things in Your law.

St. Augustine of Hippo

Speak, Lord, for Your servant is listening.

1 Samuel 3:9, NAB

All my sermons are prepared in the presence of the Blessed Sacrament. As recreation is most pleasant and profitable in the sun, so homiletic creativity is best nourished before the Eucharist. The most brilliant ideas come from meeting God face to face. The Holy Spirit that presided at the Incarnation is the best atmosphere for illumination.

Archbishop Fulton J. Sheen

Let me hear what God the Lord will speak,
for He will speak peace to His people,
to His saints, to those who turn to Him in their hearts.

PSALM 85:8

Speak, therefore, Lord, for Your servant listens. You have the words of eternal life. Speak to me for the comfort of my soul and for the amendment of my life, for Your praise, Your glory, and Your everlasting honor.

THOMAS À KEMPIS

No one must forget that the Lord, as the Master of the laborers in the vineyard, calls at every hour of life so as to make His holy will more precisely and explicitly known. Therefore, the fundamental and continuous attitude of the disciple should be one of vigilance and a conscious attentiveness to the voice of God.

POPE JOHN PAUL II

Let Truth Himself, the Light of my heart, speak to me, and not my own darkness! I had fallen into that darkness and had been blinded by it. But even there, in its depths, I came to love You, Lord. Even when I went astray, I remembered You. I heard Your voice behind me, calling me to return, though I could hardly hear it above the din of my own passions. And now, see how I am returning, burning and panting for Your fountain.... Speak to me; talk with me.

ST. AUGUSTINE OF HIPPO

For Wisdom, Before the Blessed Sacrament
Word made Flesh,
Bread made Word,
Wisdom made Food:
Speak to me.
For I am deaf
from the roar of the world
and only Your voice
can heal me.

Round white Tablet:
secrets inscribed here
tell of Your will.
Read to me.
For I am blind
in the night of the world
until Your beams
enlighten me.

PAUL THIGPEN

O Lord, my heart is not lifted up,
my eyes are not raised too high;
I do not occupy myself with things
too great and too marvelous for me.
But I have calmed and quieted my soul,
like a child quieted at its mother's breast;
like a child that is quieted is my soul.
O Israel, hope in the Lord
from this time forth and for evermore.

PSALM 131

Above all things and in all things, O my soul, rest always in God, for He is the everlasting rest of the saints.

Grant, most sweet and loving Jesus, that I may seek my repose in You above every creature; above all health and beauty; above every honor and glory; every power and dignity; above all knowledge and cleverness, all riches and arts, all joy and gladness; above all fame and praise, all sweetness and consolation; above every hope and promise, every merit and desire; above all the gifts and favors that You can give or pour down upon me; above all the joy and exultation that the mind can receive and feel; and finally, above the angels and archangels and all the heavenly host; above all things visible and invisible; and may I seek my repose in You above everything that is not You, my God.

For You, O Lord my God, are above all things the best. You alone are most high, You alone most powerful. You alone are most sufficient and most satisfying, You alone most sweet and consoling. You alone are most beautiful and loving, You alone most noble and glorious above all things. In You is every perfection that has been or ever will be. Therefore, whatever You give me besides Yourself, whatever You reveal to me concerning Yourself, and whatever You promise, is too small and insufficient when I do not see and fully enjoy You alone. For my heart cannot rest or be fully content until, rising above all gifts and every created thing, it rests in You....

O Jesus, Splendor of eternal glory, Consolation of the pilgrim soul, with You my lips utter no sound, and to You my silence speaks.

THOMAS À KEMPIS

The Lord is my shepherd, I shall not want;
    He makes me lie down in green pastures.
He leads me beside still waters;
    He restores my soul.
He leads me in the paths of righteousness
    for His name's sake.
Even though I walk
    through the valley of the shadow of death,
I fear no evil;
    for Thou art with me;
    Thy rod and Thy staff,
    they comfort me.
Thou preparest a table before me
    in the presence of my enemies;
Thou anointest my head with oil,
    my cup overflows.
Surely goodness and mercy shall follow me
    all the days of my life;
and I shall dwell in the house of the Lord
    for ever.

PSALM 23

You are great, Lord, and greatly to be praised, Your power is great, and Your wisdom is infinite. Man desires to praise You, Lord, for he is one of Your creatures. Though he bears the mark of death wherever he goes as a testimony to his sin—a reminder that You resist the proud—yet still, because man is a part of Your creation, he desires to praise You. You move us to delight in praising You, for You have made us for Yourself, and our hearts are restless till they find their rest in You.

ST. AUGUSTINE OF HIPPO

Sometimes You speak, Lord,
in tongues so strange
that I must pray
for grace to obey
without understanding.

Sometimes You sing
such a lovely song
that I must laugh
at the silly tune
I thought was wisdom.

Sometimes You shout
in a voice so loud
that I must awake
and confess again
that I was sleeping.

But in this moment
when silence is Your word to me
and stillness is my prayer
I rest within a confidence
born in the quiet of Your smile:
I am beloved.

PAUL THIGPEN

Most gracious Lord Jesus, grant me above all things that can be desired that I may rest in You fully, that You may bring peace to my heart. You, Lord, are the most true peace of the heart, the perfect rest of body and soul. Without You, all things weary and disturb. So in that peace which is in You—the one high, blessed, endless Goodness—I will always find my rest. Amen.

THOMAS À KEMPIS

At that time Jesus declared,... "Come to Me, all who labor and are heavy laden, and I will give you rest. Take My yoke upon you, and learn from Me; for I am gentle and lowly in heart, and you will find rest for your souls. For My yoke is easy, and My burden is light."

MATTHEW 11:25, 28-30

Grant us, Lord God, Your peace: for You have supplied us with all things. Give us the peace of quietness, the peace of the Sabbath, the peace without an evening to end it. For all this most beautiful order of things in Your creation, all so very good, must nevertheless pass away, their courses being finished—for You made them to have a morning and evening. But the seventh day, the day of our final rest, is without any evening, nor does the sun ever set on it—for You have sanctified it to last forever.

ST. AUGUSTINE OF HIPPO

For thus says the Lord God, the Holy One of Israel,
"In returning and rest you shall be saved;
in quietness and trust shall be your strength...."
Therefore the Lord waits to be gracious to you;
therefore he exalts himself to show mercy to you.

Isaiah 30:15, 18

SIX

"HIS HANDS FULL OF GRACES"
Petition
Coming to Jesus With Our Needs

Our Lord in the Blessed Sacrament has His hands
full of graces, and He is ready to bestow them on
anyone who asks for them.

ST. PETER OF ALCANTARA

He who eats my flesh and drinks my blood abides in me, and
I in him.... If you abide in me, and my words abide in you,
ask whatever you will, and it shall be done for you.

JOHN 6:56; 15:7

Pierce, O most sweet Lord Jesus, my inmost soul with the most
joyous and healthful wound of Your love, with truly serene and
most apostolic charity, that my soul may ever languish and
melt with love and longing for You, that it may yearn for You
and faint for Your courts, and long to be dissolved and to be
with You. Grant that my soul may hunger after You, the Bread
of angels, the Refreshment of holy souls, our daily and supersubstantial Bread having all sweetness and savor and every
delight of taste.

Let my heart ever hunger after and feed upon You, upon whom the angels desire to look, and may my inmost soul be filled with the sweetness of Your savor. May my soul ever thirst after You, the Fountain of life, the Fountain of wisdom and knowledge, the Fountain of eternal Light, the Torrent of pleasure, the Richness of the house of God.

May it ever compass You, seek You, find You, run to You, attain You, meditate upon You, speak of You and do all things to the praise and glory of Your name; with humility and discretion, with love and delight, with ease and affection, and with perseverance unto the end.

May You alone be ever my hope, my entire assurance, my riches, my delight, my pleasure, my joy, my rest and tranquility, my peace, my sweetness, my fragrance, my sweet savor, my food, my refreshment, my refuge, my help, my wisdom, my portion, my possession and my treasure, in whom may my mind and my heart be fixed and firm and rooted immovably henceforth and forever. Amen.

ST. BONAVENTURE

I sought the Lord, and he answered me,
and delivered me from all my fears.
Look to him, and be radiant;
so your faces shall never be ashamed.
This poor man cried, and the Lord heard him,
and saved him out of all his troubles.

PSALM 34:4-6

Give me the grace to long for Your holy sacraments, and especially to rejoice in the presence of Your Body, sweet Savior Christ, in the holy Sacrament of the altar. Amen.

St. Thomas More

To converse with You, O King of glory, no third person is needed, You are always ready in the Sacrament of the altar to give audience to all. All who desire You always find You there, and converse with You face to face.

St. Teresa of Avila

Ask, and it will be given you; seek, and you will find; knock, and it will be opened to you. For every one who asks receives, and he who seeks finds, and to him who knocks it will be opened. Or what man of you, if his son asks him for bread, will give him a stone? Or if he asks for a fish, will give him a serpent? If you then, who are evil, know how to give good gifts to your children, how much more will your Father who is in heaven give good things to those who ask him!

Matthew 7:7-11

Like the sick who expose their diseased bodies to the healing rays of the sun, expose miseries, no matter what they are, to the beams of light streaming forth from the sacred Host.

José Guadalupe Trevino

O good Jesus, hear me. Never permit me to be separated from You. From the evil one protect me, at the hour of death call me, and bid me to come to You so that with Your saints I may praise You forever. Amen.

God likes to listen favorably to the prayers of His faithful, particularly when they are looking at Christ's Body.

WILLIAM OF AUXERRE

How sweet is the moment in which poor humanity, wearied and afflicted, may remain alone, with Jesus alone, in the Sacrament of love; for there the Lord, with His flaming heart open, calls unto all, "You that are burdened and heavy laden, come unto Me and I will refresh you." Happy are those hearts that know how to satisfy the unquenchable hunger and thirst in this heavenly Banquet!

FR. M.J. CORCORAN, O.S.A.

Good Lord, teach me to be generous. Teach me to serve You as You deserve; to give, and not to count the cost; to fight, and not to heed the wounds; to labor, and not to seek rest; to give of myself, and not to ask for reward, except the reward of knowing that I am doing Your will.

Take, O Lord, and receive my entire liberty, my memory, my understanding, and my whole will. All that I am, all that I have, You have given to me, and I will give it back to You to be disposed of according to Your good pleasure.

Give me Your love and Your graces; with You I am rich enough, nor do I ask for anything besides. Amen.

ST. IGNATIUS LOYOLA

Give me Yourself, O my God, give Yourself to me. Behold I love You, and if my love is too weak a thing, grant me to love You more strongly. I cannot measure my love to know how much it falls short of being sufficient, but let my soul hasten to Your embrace and never be turned away until it is hidden in the secret shelter of Your presence. This only do I know, that it is not good for me when You are not with me, when You are only outside me. I want You in my very self. All the plenty in the world that is not my God is poverty. Amen.

ST. AUGUSTINE OF HIPPO

When we go before the Blessed Sacrament, let us open our heart; our good God will open His. We shall go to Him; He will come to us; the one to ask, the other to receive. It will be like a breath from one to the other.

ST. JOHN VIANNEY

Soul of Christ, sanctify me.
Body of Christ, save me.
Blood of Christ, inebriate me.
Water from the side of Christ, wash me.
Passion of Christ, strengthen me.
O good Jesus, hear me.
Within Thy wounds hide me.
Permit me not to be separated from Thee.
From the wicked foe defend me.
At the hour of my death call me
and bid me come to Thee
that with Thy saints I may praise Thee
forever and ever. Amen.

To speak of the Blessed Sacrament is to speak of what is most sacred. How often, when we are in a state of distress, those to whom we look for help leave us—or what is worse, add to our affliction by heaping fresh troubles upon us. He is ever there waiting to help us.

ST. EUPHRASIA PELLETIER

Great God, hear my prayers! Oh, that I could breathe my last before Your tabernacle, burning with love and bathed with my tears!

ST. GERTRUDE THE GREAT

Act of Spiritual Communion

A spiritual communion, according to St. Thomas, consists in an ardent desire to receive Jesus in the Most Holy Sacrament, and in lovingly embracing Him as if we had actually received Him. All those who desire to advance in the love of Jesus Christ are exhorted to make a spiritual communion at least once every visit that they pay to the Most Blessed Sacrament. This devotion is far more profitable than some suppose, and at the same time nothing can be easier to practice.

ST. ALPHONSUS LIGUORI

My Jesus, I believe that You are truly present in the Most Blessed Sacrament. I love You above all things, and I desire to possess You within my soul. Since I am unable now to receive You sacramentally, come at least spiritually into my heart. I embrace You as if You were already there, and I unite myself wholly to You; never permit me to be separated from You. Amen.

ST. ALPHONSUS LIGUORI

What does Jesus Christ do in the Eucharist? It is God who, as our Savior, offers Himself each day for us to His Father's justice. If you are in difficulties and sorrows, He will comfort and relieve you. If you are sick, He will either cure you or give you strength to suffer so as to merit heaven. If the devil, the world, and the flesh are making war upon you, He will give you the weapons with which to fight, to resist and to win victory. If you are poor, He will enrich you with all sorts of riches for time and eternity. Let us open the door of His sacred and adorable Heart, and be wrapped about for an instant by the flames of His love, and we shall see what a God who loves us can do.

ST. JOHN VIANNEY

Nowhere does Jesus hear our prayers more readily than in the Blessed Sacrament.

BLESSED HENRY SUSO

Through Eucharistic adoration we concentrate our attention on Him as we yield to the fascination of His invisible gaze. Opening our heart, we entrust all our petitions to Him.

JEAN GALOT, S.J.

It is for us that, during eighteen hundred years, our divine Savior has remained day and night on our altars, that we may have recourse to Him in all our needs; and nothing so much afflicts His divine Heart as our ingratitude for such a favor, and our neglect to visit Him and ask His blessing. If we knew how profitable those visits are, we should be constantly prostrate before the altar. The saints understood this truth; they knew that Jesus Christ is the Source of all grace, and whenever they encountered any difficulty or wished to obtain any particular favor, they ran to Jesus Christ in the Blessed Sacrament.

BLESSED J.B. MARCELLIN CHAMPAGNAT

So learn to pray to God in such a way that you are trusting Him as your Physician to do what He knows is best. Confess to Him the disease, and let Him choose the remedy. Then hold tight to love, for what He does will cut and sting you. You may cry out, and your cries may not stop the cutting, the burning, and the pain; yet He knows how deep the festering flesh lies. While you want Him to take His hands off you, He considers only the extent of the infection; He knows how far He must go. He is not listening to you according to what you want, but according to what will heal you.

ST. AUGUSTINE OF HIPPO

Litany of the Most Blessed Sacrament

Lord, have mercy; Lord, have mercy.

Christ, have mercy; Christ, have mercy.

Lord, have mercy; Lord, have mercy.

Christ, hear us; Christ, hear us.

Christ, graciously hear us; Christ, graciously hear us.

    God the Father of Heaven, have mercy on us.

    God the Son, Redeemer of the world, have mercy on us.

    God the Holy Spirit, have mercy on us.

    Holy Trinity, one God, have mercy on us.

O living Bread, who from heaven descended, have mercy on us.

Hidden God and Savior, have mercy on us.

Grain of the elect, have mercy on us.

Vine sprouting forth virgins, have mercy on us.

Wholesome Bread and Delicacy of kings, have mercy on us.

    Perpetual Sacrifice, have mercy on us.

    Clean Oblation, have mercy on us.

    Lamb without spot, have mercy on us.

    Purest Banquet, have mercy on us.

    Food of angels, have mercy on us.

Hidden Manna, have mercy on us.

Memorial of God's wonders, have mercy on us.

Supersubstantial Bread, have mercy on us.

Word made flesh, living in us, have mercy on us.

Holy Victim, have mercy on us.

    O Cup of blessing, have mercy on us.

    O Mystery of faith, have mercy on us.

    O most high and venerable Sacrament, have mercy on us.

    O Most Holy of all sacrifices, have mercy on us.

    O true propitiatory Sacrifice for the living
       and the dead, have mercy on us.

    O heavenly Antidote, by which we are preserved from sin,
       have mercy on us.

    O stupendous Miracle above all others, have mercy on us.

    O most holy Commemoration of the passion of Christ,
       have mercy on us.

    O Gift transcending all abundance, have mercy on us.

    O extraordinary Memorial of divine love,
       have mercy on us.

    O Affluence of divine largess, have mercy on us.

    O most holy and august Mystery, have mercy on us.

Medicine of immortality, have mercy on us.

Awesome and life-giving Sacrament, have mercy on us.

Unbloody Sacrifice, have mercy on us.

Food and Guest, have mercy on us.

Sweetest Feast at which the angels serve,
    have mercy on us.

Bond of love, have mercy on us.

Offering and Oblation, have mercy on us.

Spiritual Sweetness tasted in its own fountain,
    have mercy on us.

Refreshment of holy souls, have mercy on us.

Viaticum of those dying in the Lord, have mercy on us.

Pledge of future glory, have mercy on us.

Be merciful, spare us, O Lord.

Be merciful, hear us, O Lord.

> From the unworthy reception of Your Body and Blood,
> deliver us, O Lord.

> From passions of the flesh, deliver us, O Lord.

> From the concupiscence of the eyes,
> deliver us, O Lord.

> From pride, deliver us, O Lord.

> From every occasion of sin, deliver us, O Lord.

Through that desire, with which You desired to eat the
Passover with Your disciples, deliver us, O Lord.

Through that profound humility with which You washed Your
disciples' feet, deliver us, O Lord.

Through that most ardent love, with which You instituted this
divine Sacrament, deliver us, O Lord.

Through the most precious Blood, which You have left for us
upon the altar, deliver us, O Lord.

Through those five wounds of Your most holy Body, which was
given up for us, deliver us, O Lord.

Sinners we are, we ask You, hear us.

That You would graciously preserve and augment the faith,
reverence, and devotion in us towards this admirable
Sacrament, we ask You, hear us.

That You would graciously lead us through the true
confession of our sins to a frequent reception of the
Eucharist, we ask You, hear us.

That You would graciously free us from every heresy,
falsehood, and blindness of the heart,
we ask You, hear us.

That You would graciously impart to us the heavenly

and precious fruits of this most holy Sacrament,
we ask You, hear us.

That You would graciously protect and strengthen us
in our hour of death with this heavenly Viaticum,
we ask You, hear us.

O Son of God, we ask You, hear us.

Lamb of God, who takes away the sins of the world,
spare us, O Lord.

Lamb of God, who takes away the sins of the world,
graciously hear us, O Lord.

Lamb of God, who takes away the sins of the world,
have mercy on us, O Lord.

Christ, hear us; Christ, hear us.

Christ, graciously hear us; Christ, graciously hear us.

Lord, have mercy; Lord, have mercy.

Christ, have mercy; Christ, have mercy.

Lord, have mercy; Lord, have mercy.

Our Father ...

Hail Mary ...

You furnished them with Bread from heaven,
Having in it all sweetness.

Let us pray. O God, who under a marvelous Sacrament has left us a memorial of Your Passion, grant us, we beseech You, so to venerate the sacred Mysteries of Your Body and Blood, that we may ever perceive within us the fruit of Your Redemption. You, who live and reign forever and ever. Amen.

MANUALE SACERDOTUM, P. JOSEPHUS SCHNEIDER, S.J.;

FOR PRIVATE USE ONLY

SEVEN

"THE MOST BEAUTIFUL OF ALL MISSIONS"
Intercession and Reparation
Praying for Others

Eucharistic adorers share Mary's life and mission of prayer at the foot of the Most Blessed Sacrament. It is the most beautiful of all missions, and it holds no perils.

ST. PETER JULIAN EYMARD

First of all, then, I urge that supplications, prayers, intercessions, and thanksgivings be made for all men.... This is good, and it is acceptable in the sight of God our Savior, who desires all men to be saved and to come to the knowledge of the truth. For there is one God, and there is one mediator between God and men, the man Christ Jesus, who gave himself as a ransom for all.

1 TIMOTHY 1, 3-4

We would all much better mend our ways if we were as ready to pray for one another as we are to offer one another reproach and rebuke.

ST. THOMAS MORE

And since so few people now hear the words, "Come to Me, all you who labor and are burdened," let each of us, when he approaches the holy table, look upon himself as the delegate of all those he loves or has loved, living or dead. When God makes His way into our souls, He does not find us alone. All those from whom we proceed and who have gone to sleep before us may receive, in purgatory, some benefit of grace pervading us, their living children, when we pray for them. And all our friends who are kept away from the Source of grace by sin, indifference, ignorance, and incredulity—those who have helped us and those we have harmed—are present in our thoughts in this ineffable instant.

FRANÇOIS MAURIAC

O living Host, my one and only Strength, Fountain of love and mercy, embrace the whole world, and fortify faint souls!

ST. FAUSTINA KOWALSKA

In Reparation

In the most Blessed Sacrament, Christ, the glorious King of angels and of men, our good Lord, adores, appeases, and satisfies the justice of His Father, offers Him His past sufferings, His present humiliations, His poverty, His obedience, and His love to compensate for the injury, for the crime, for the ingratitude, and for the sins that are rampant in the world. Come and unite your meager atonement to that of the Divine One, and you will be made clean and pleasing to God. Come and make reparation for your sins and the sins of the world.

ST. PETER JULIAN EYMARD

Our hours of adoration will be special hours of reparation for sins, and intercession for the needs of the whole world, exposing the sin-sick and suffering humanity to the healing, sustaining, and transforming rays of Jesus radiating from the Eucharist.

MOTHER TERESA OF CALCUTTA

O Most Holy Trinity, Father, Son, and Holy Spirit, I adore Thee profoundly. I offer Thee the most precious Body, Blood, Soul, and Divinity of Jesus Christ, present in all the tabernacles of the world, in reparation for the outrages, sacrileges, and indifference by which He is offended. By the infinite merits of the Sacred Heart of Jesus and the Immaculate Heart of Mary, I beg the conversion of poor sinners. Amen.

ANGEL'S PRAYER AT FATIMA

For the Dying

Most merciful Eucharistic Jesus, Lover of souls, I pray Thee, by the agony of Thy Most Sacred Heart and by the sorrows of Thine Immaculate Mother, to wash in Thy most precious Blood the sinners of the world who are now in their agony, and who will die today. Heart of Jesus, once in agony, have mercy on the dying. Amen.

For the City

Look down, O Lord, from Your sanctuary, from Your dwelling in heaven on high, and behold this sacred Victim which our great High Priest, Your holy Son our Lord Jesus Christ, offers up to You for the sins of His brethren, and be appeased despite the multitude of our transgressions. Behold, the voice of the Blood of Jesus, our Brother, cries to You from the cross.

Give ear, O Lord. Be appeased, O Lord. Hearken and do not delay for Your own sake, O my God; for Your Name is invoked upon this city and upon Your people; and deal with us according to Your mercy. Amen. That You would defend, pacify, keep, preserve, and bless this city, we beseech You, hear us.

ST. CAJETAN

For Enemies and Persecutors

Almighty God, have mercy on *(name)* and all who bear an evil will toward me, and who wish to harm me; by the kind of gentle, tender, merciful means that Your infinite wisdom can best devise, grant to correct and redress both their faults and mine together, and make us saved souls in heaven together, where we may ever live and love together with You and Your blessed saints, O glorious Trinity, for the bitter Passion of our sweet Savior Christ. Amen.

ST. THOMAS MORE

For Souls in Purgatory

O gentlest Heart of Jesus, ever present in the Blessed Sacrament, ever consumed with burning love for the poor captive souls in purgatory, have mercy on the soul of Your departed servant *(name)*. Be not severe in Your judgment, but let some drops of the precious Blood fall upon the devouring flames, O merciful Savior, and send Your angels to conduct Your departed servant to a place of refreshment, light, and peace. Amen.

Grant them eternal rest, O Lord. May perpetual light shine upon them. May their souls and the souls of all the faithful departed, through the mercy of God, rest in peace. Amen.

Jesu, by that shuddering dread which fell on Thee;
Jesu, by that cold dismay which sicken'd Thee;
Jesu, by that pang of heart which thrilled in Thee;
Jesu, by that mount of sins which crippled Thee;
Jesu, by that sense of guilt which stifled Thee;
Jesu, by that innocence which girdled Thee;
Jesu, by that sanctity which reigned in Thee;
Jesu, by that Godhead which was one with Thee;
Jesu, spare these souls which are so dear to Thee;
who in prison, calm and patient, wait for Thee;
Hasten, Lord, their hour, and bid them come to Thee,
to that glorious home, where they shall ever gaze on Thee.

VENERABLE JOHN HENRY NEWMAN

For the Church

O Lord, save Thy people, and bless Thine inheritance; govern them, and lift them up forever; day by day we magnify Thee, and we worship Thy name, ever world without end. Amen.

THE DIVINE OFFICE

For the Unity of the Church

When Jesus had spoken these words, He lifted up his eyes to heaven and said,... "Holy Father, keep them in Thy name, which Thou hast given me, that they may be one, even as We are one.... I do not pray for these only, but also for those who believe in Me through their word.... The glory which Thou hast given me I have given to them, that they may be one even as We are one, I in them and Thou in Me, that they may become perfectly one, so that the world may know thatThou hast sent Me and hast loved them even as Thou hast loved me."

JOHN 17:1, 11, 15-23

Where charity and love are, God is there;
    Christ's love has gathered us into one.
Let us rejoice and be pleased in Him;
    let us fear and let us love the living God;
    and let us love Him with a sincere heart.
As we are gathered into one Body, beware,
    lest we be divided in mind.
Let evil dissension stop, let controversy cease,
    and may Christ be in our midst.
And may we also with the saints
    gloriously see Your face, O Christ,
The joy that is infinite and good,
    forever and ever. Amen.

FROM THE LITURGY FOR HOLY THURSDAY

For the Holy Father in Rome

Lord Jesus Christ, reigning from Your Eucharistic throne, establish the throne of Your vicar, our Holy Father, Pope *(name)*, in faithfulness, justice, truth, and peace. Uphold him, defend him, enlighten him, console him, enliven him with all graces to lead Your Church boldly in Your footsteps and to gather together into one flock those who look to You for salvation. Amen.

Litany for Priests

Jesus, meek and humble of heart,
    give all priests Thy spirit of humility;
Jesus, poor and worn out for souls,
    give all priests Thy spirit of zeal;
Jesus, full of patience and mercy for sinners,
    give all priests Thy spirit of compassion;

Jesus, victim for the sins of the world,
    give all priests Thy spirit of sacrifice;
Jesus, lover of the little and the poor,
    give all priests Thy spirit of charity.
Mary, Queen of the Clergy, pray for us; and obtain for us
    numerous and holy priests and religious. Amen.

For Missions

Eternal Father, it is Your will that all should be saved. Great is Your mercy. Your Son, Jesus Christ, died for all. Teach all people to recognize You and love You. With deep faith in Christ's death and resurrection we pray: Send forth, O Lord, laborers into Your vineyard and spare Your people.

Eternal Word, Redeemer of all creation, convert all souls to You. You have been obedient for all, even to death on the cross. Look upon the merits of Your Mother and of all the angels and saints who intercede for us. Send forth, O Lord, laborers into Your vineyard and spare Your people.

O Holy Spirit, through the infinite merits of our Lord Jesus Christ, enkindle in all hearts Your ardent love that can do all things, that all may be one fold under one Shepherd, and that all may arrive in heaven to sing Your divine mercy.

Queen of Apostles and all the angels and saints, pray to the Lord of the harvest: Send forth, O Lord, laborers into Your vineyard and spare Your people, that united with You, and the Father and the Holy Spirit, we may all rejoice forever. Amen.

St. Vincent Pallotti

For Peace

Almighty and eternal God, may Your grace enkindle in all of us a love for the many unfortunate people whom poverty and misery reduce to a condition of life unworthy of human beings. Arouse in the hearts of those who call You Father a hunger and thirst for social justice and for fraternal charity in deeds and in truth. Grant, O Lord, peace in our days, peace to souls, peace to families, peace to our country, and peace among nations. Amen.

POPE PIUS XII

For the Poor

And Mary said,
"My soul magnifies the Lord!...
He has scattered the proud in the imagination of their hearts,
He has put down the mighty from their thrones,
and exalted those of low degree;
He has filled the hungry with good things,
and the rich He has sent empty away."

LUKE 1:46, 51-54

Lord Jesus, what has made You so small?
Love.

ST. BERNARD OF CLAIRVAUX

For the "Little People," Before the Blessed Sacrament

Tiny round God,
weak and small, You could fit in my hand, yet
all the span of the universe cannot contain You
all the powers of the cosmos cannot resist You.
You have made Yourself like those
who are close to Your Heart.

I carry them here with me today:
the "little people"
invisible to the mighty but not to the Almighty.
The world reckons them a zero:
without wealth, without power,
without name, without face,
without arms, without voice.

But You too, Lord, are a Zero,
a white, wheaten Cipher,
a Figure on whom
they have failed to reckon.

When Your foes seek to multiply
You will invade their equation
and bring them to naught:
You will nullify their pride,
annihilate their power,
annul their schemes
of domination.
But those of lowly degree
You will stand beside
to magnify.

Tiny round God,
blessed are You
who gather the poor
into the ring of Your riches,
the empty
into the cup of Your fullness,
the weak
into the crown of Your might,
the sorrowing
into the circle of Your dance.
Blessed are You,
encompassing Your people
without beginning, without end,
in Your love.

PAUL THIGPEN

For All in Need

O living Bread, who came down from heaven to give life to the world! O loving Shepherd of our souls, a hidden God, who pours out from Your throne of glory Your grace on families and peoples, we commend to You particularly the sick, the unhappy, the poor, and all who beg for food and employment, imploring for all and everyone the assistance of Your providence; we commend to You the families, so that they may be fruitful centers of Christian life. May the abundance of Your grace be poured out over all.

BLESSED POPE JOHN XXIII

EIGHT

"A CONCERT OF PRAYER"
Solidarity
Joining With the Angels and Saints

A holy rivalry, a concert of prayer, a harmony of divine service, should exist between the heavenly court and the Eucharistic court here below, between the adorer and his mother the Church.

ST. PETER JULIAN EYMARD

After this I heard what seemed to be the mighty voice of a great multitude in heaven, crying, *"Hallelujah! Salvation and glory and power belong to our God, for his judgments are true and just."* ...

And from the throne came a voice crying, *"Praise our God, all you his servants, you who fear him, small and great."*

Then I heard what seemed to be the voice of a great multitude, like the sound of many waters and like the sound of mighty thunderpeals, crying, *"Hallelujah! For the Lord our God the Almighty reigns. Let us rejoice and exult and give him the glory."*

REVELATION 19:1-2, 5-7

O glorious Blessed Trinity, may I through the merits of Christ's bitter passion be a partner in Your blessedness with those holy spirits who stood faithful to You and, now confirmed by Your grace, will stand forever in glory.

ST. THOMAS MORE

To the Holy Angels

*O holy angels, make me see God on the altar
as you see Him in heaven.*

BLESSED ANDRÉ BESSETTE

This Fountain [of the Blessed Sacrament] is a fountain of light, shedding abundant rays of truth. And beside it the angelic powers from on high have taken their stand, gazing on the beauty of its streams, since they perceive more clearly than we the power of what lies before us and its unapproachable dazzling rays.

ST. JOHN CHRYSOSTOM

Eternal Son of the living God, whom I acknowledge here as truly present, I adore You with all the powers of my soul! Prostrate with the angels in the most profound reverence, I love You, O my Savior, whom I now behold on Your throne of love. O dread Majesty, O infinite Mercy, save me! Forgive me! Grant that I may never more be separated from You!

ST. BASIL THE GREAT

To the Holy Angels, Before the Blessed Sacrament

You glorious morning stars!
whose shout of joy shook heaven when God's masterpiece was
    done;
who grieved to see your conquered foes become our conquerors,
who sorrowed at our exile as you closed the gate to Eden.

You armament of God!
who robbed the sons from Egypt and turned back the towering
    waves;
who kept a Sinai vigil to preserve a careless people
playing in the dust beside the den where ancient Serpent
    coiled.

You swift, sure-flying heralds!
who bore the burning words of God that seared the stones of
    Law
and pierced the breasts of Prophets with a Father's sharp lament
and filled a Nation's souls with longing for the reign of God.

You shining troubadours!
whose splendor danced through desert skies to welcome God
    to earth;
whose warning stole the lion's prey until the time appointed;
who wiped the sweat from off the Face you once adored in
    glory.

You stout celestial soldiers!
who silent stood, ten thousand strong, and watched the
crime of ages,
unmoved because unbidden by your Captain to resist;
yet ready when He gave command to hurl the stone away.

You firm and patient teachers!
who drew the curtain on the Flesh ascended now in glory
and chided men for skyward glances focused on the clouds
and promised He would come again when faith gives way to
sight.

My morning stars!
Your joy still flames to see his Image, marred but real, in me.
Your silent grief still spills to see me banished, vanquished,
broken.

My armament!
Your whispered thoughts of wisdom come to rob me of my
folly;
your vigil still protects me in the wild wastes of my will.

My heralds!
You sear this stony heart and pierce this breast and leave me
longing
for the Word of God imprisoned in this silent, suffering
Host.

My troubadours!
Your hidden splendor welcomes God again to His enclosure
as you crowd beside me worshipping divine Humility.

My soldiers!

Still strong in silent patience as your Captain stays your
   vengeance

while the day of visitation slips away before the Judgment.

My teachers!

You hold the curtain still across the Flesh that hides before
   me,

where my God appears as bread until my faith gives way to
   sight:

Keep me gazing on the One who came, who comes, and
   who will come.

PAUL THIGPEN

Bless the Lord, O you his angels,
you mighty ones who do his word,
hearkening to the voice of his word!
Bless the Lord, all his hosts,
his ministers that do his will!

PSALM 103:20-21

Angel of God, my guardian dear,
to whom his love commits me here,
ever this day be at my side
to light and guard, to rule and guide.
Amen.

O glorious Blessed Trinity, whose justice has damned to perpetual pain many proud, rebellious angels,... for the sake of Your tender mercy, plant in my heart such meekness that I may by Your grace follow the promptings of my guardian angel, and resist the proud suggestions of those spiteful spirits who fell.

ST. THOMAS MORE

To My Guardian Angel, Before the Blessed Sacrament
My Guardian,
Hold my hand lest, over-timid,
    I should flee so great a Sovereignty.
Prick my heart lest, too familiar,
    I insult so great a Clemency.
Fix my eyes lest, too distracted,
    I grow blind to such a Majesty.
Move my tongue lest, too lethargic,
    I neglect such opportunity.

PAUL THIGPEN

O glorious guardian of my soul!
You who shine brilliantly in God's great heaven,
as a sweet and pure flame,
near the throne of the Eternal One!
You come down to earth for my sake
and, illuminating me with your splendor,
you become my brother, dear angel,

my friend and comfort....
The kingdom and the glory are yours,
the riches of the King of kings;
but the Host in the humble ciborium belongs to me,
and all the treasures of the cross.

ST. THÉRÈSE OF LISIEUX

St. Michael, the archangel, defend us in battle. Be our protection against the wickedness and snares of the devil. May God rebuke him, we humbly pray, and do thou, O prince of the heavenly hosts, by the power of God thrust into hell Satan and all the other evil spirits who prowl about the world seeking the ruin of souls. Amen.

To St. Michael, Before the Blessed Sacrament
St. Michael,
though demons tremble at this Bread,
this Host their hosts dismay,
my darkened heart, I fear, may prove
their refuge from the Light.
St. Michael,
stand guard not just before His Throne
but by my will as well
lest Legion, leering, creep too close
and stain the royal shadow.

PAUL THIGPEN

Glorious St. Michael, prince of the heavenly hosts, who stands always ready to give assistance to the people of God; who fought with the dragon, the old serpent, and cast him out of heaven, and now valiantly defends the Church of God that the gates of hell may never prevail against her, I earnestly entreat you to assist me also, in the painful and dangerous conflict which I sustain against the same formidable foe.

Be with me, O mighty prince! that I may courageously fight and vanquish that proud spirit, whom you, by the Divine Power, gloriously overthrew, and whom our powerful King, Jesus Christ, has, in our nature, completely overcome; so having triumphed over the enemy of my salvation, I may with you and the holy angels praise the mercy of God who, having refused mercy to the rebellious angels after their fall, has granted repentance and forgiveness to fallen man. Amen.

To St. Raphael, Before the Blessed Sacrament
St. Raphael,
   my spirit is fainting,
   my soul is wounded,
   my mind is poisoned,
   my heart is bruised,
   my will is fevered,
   my flesh is weak.
My enemies have assaulted me,
   and I am my greatest enemy.

Yet the Sun of righteousness
rises in this room
with healing in His wings;

the burning Bush kindles
to cauterize wounds;
the Spring of living water
flows to quench fever;
the Medicine of immortality
holds cure and antidote;
the Tree of life spreads out His limbs
with fruit and shade.

St. Raphael,
window of the Sunlight,
torch of the Flame,
cup of the Fountain,
jar of the Balm,
basket of the Fruit,
breeze of the Shade,
come to my side:
I wait to be healed.

PAUL THIGPEN

To the Archangel Gabriel, Before the Blessed Sacrament
St. Gabriel,
echo of God's mind,
haunter of dreams,
trumpet of destinies,
bard of the Morning!

Behold, in this place
the Dawn you declared
has come:

tiny Daystar,
Eye of Heaven,
blazing white,
daunting the darkness.
The Virgin you hailed
has given a Son,
and the Son
has given His Flesh.

St. Gabriel,
faithful herald,
come sing with me
of promises kept,
of prophecies fulfilled.

St. Gabriel,
winged wisdom,
come speak to me
of wonders wrought,
of God's own Word
abiding.

PAUL THIGPEN

To the Blessed Virgin Mary

The piety of the Christian people has always very rightly sensed a profound link between devotion to the Blessed Virgin and worship of the Eucharist: This is a fact that can be seen in the liturgy of both the West and East, in the traditions of religious families, in the modern movements of spirituality, including those of youth, and in the pastoral practice of Marian shrines. Mary guides the faithful to the Eucharist.

POPE JOHN PAUL II

Hail, O true Body, born of the Virgin Mary, and which for man was sacrificed upon the cross! Be blessed, O holy Virgin, through whom we received the heavenly Bread that preserves and increases true life within us!

Don't you see our Lady always beside the tabernacle?

BLESSED PADRE PIO

O Mary, Mother of Jesus Christ, and our dear Mother! O all you holy angels, who by your adoration in our churches make up for the meager love that your God, our Savior, receives from men: Obtain for us the grace to understand even a little the love of Jesus Christ in the Most Holy Sacrament.

ST. MARGARET MARY ALACOQUE

When we go before Jesus on the altar, we always find Him with Mary His Mother, as the Magi did at Bethlehem (See Mt 2:11). And Jesus in the sacred Host, from the altar of our hearts, can repeat to each one of us what He said to St. John the Evangelist from the altar of Calvary, *Behold thy Mother* (See Jn 19:27).

FR. STEFANO MANELLI, O.F.M.

Beneath the Eucharist's sacramental veils is the living fruit of Mary's womb.

FR. RICHARD FOLEY, S.J.

Hail, most holy Virgin, burning bush which without being consumed held the fire of divinity! Hail, spiritual oven, which provided fire and the Bread of Life freshly baked for the food of the world, the food of which Christ the Savior of the world said: Take and eat, this is My body, which is broken for you unto the remission of sins. Sumptuous indeed, dearly beloved, and filled with every virtue is that virginal banquet table, laden with all best foods that rejoice the earth. The holy Virgin, the Mother of Christ, herself has furnished it.

FROM THE BREVIARY

O Mary, Immaculate Virgin,... [Jesus] descended from heaven, leaving His eternal throne, and took Body and Blood of your heart and for nine months lay hidden in a virgin's heart. O Mother, Virgin, purest of all lilies, your heart was Jesus' first tabernacle on earth.

ST. FAUSTINA KOWALSKA

United to the Divinity in the Eucharist there is Jesus' Body and Blood taken from the body and blood of the Blessed Virgin.... The flesh of Jesus is the maternal flesh of Mary, the blood of Jesus is the maternal blood of Mary. Therefore it will never be possible to separate Jesus from Mary.

FR. STEFANO MANELLI, O.F.M. CONV.

Virgin Immaculate, Mother of Jesus and our Mother, we invoke you under the title of Our Lady of the Most Blessed Sacrament because you are the Mother of the Savior who lives in the Eucharist. It was from you He took the flesh and blood with which He feeds us in the Sacred Host. We also invoke you under that title because the grace of the Eucharist comes to us through you, since you are the Mediatrix, the channel, through which God's graces reach us.

And, finally, we call you Our Lady of the Blessed Sacrament because you were the first to live the Eucharistic life. Teach us to pray the Mass as you did, to receive Holy Communion worthily and frequently, and to visit devoutly with our Lord in the Blessed Sacrament.

FR. LAWRENCE G. LOVASIK

Praying the Rosary Before the Blessed Sacrament

When we pray the rosary in front of the Blessed Sacrament, we love Jesus with the heart of Mary. When we pray the rosary in front of Jesus in the Blessed Sacrament, we offer to Jesus the perfect adoration of Mary.

We unite our love for Jesus to the perfect love and praise of Mary. Jesus receives our holy hour as if Mary herself were making it, because no matter how weak our faith or poor our love, Mary encloses us in her heart and Jesus accepts our hour with Him as coming directly from the heart of His very own Mother. The Immaculate Heart of Mary repairs and makes up for what is lacking in our own heart.

The fifteen mysteries of the rosary are related and centered in the one central mystery of our faith, the Holy Eucharist, where "the work of our redemption is accomplished." The

Eucharist continues and makes present the fifteen mysteries of the rosary.

FR. MARTIN LUCIA, S.S. C.C.

O Mary of the Rosary, keep me recollected when I say these prayers of yours; bind me forever, with your rosary, to Jesus of the Blessed Sacrament. Blessed be Jesus, my love; blessed be the Immaculate Virgin Mary!

BLESSED POPE JOHN XXIII

Adoring [Jesus'] Presence exposed on the altar or in the tabernacle, we bask in His warmth. Meditating on the rosary, we recall Jesus' life, death, and resurrection and the union of His Mother in the work of our salvation. Through the Eucharist and the rosary, two hearts are joined in love, and we, in love, are joined to those two hearts.

MICHAEL SIX

To St. Joseph

To St. Joseph, Before the Blessed Sacrament
St. Joseph, as I kneel here in wonder,
I need a measure of your faith
to deny the deceit of appearances,
to embrace the humility of God.
How else could I believe,
as you had to believe,

that Omnipotence would make Himself frail,
Infinity would make Himself small,
Eternity would bow Himself gladly
to the whims of time?
With mortal eyes like yours
I gaze on Immortality Himself,
the I AM, the Ancient of Days;
and though the sight should slay me,
I live to tell the miracle of grace.
St. Joseph, patron of all who adore a hidden God,
pray for me.

PAUL THIGPEN

St. Joseph believed unhesitatingly in the mystery of the Incarnation, in the fruitful virginity and in the divine maternity of Mary. He believed without seeing the miracles that were to fill Judea with His glory and renown of His holy name. We too should recognize Jesus in the frail Host that is offered to us at the altar. Here He is even smaller than at Bethlehem, more hidden than in St. Joseph's workshop. Still it is He.

BISHOP PETER ANASTASIUS PICHENOT

Of old the patriarch Joseph stored up food not only for himself but for all the people. St. Joseph received the living Bread come down from heaven and guarded it, both for himself and for the whole world.

ST. BERNARD OF CLAIRVAUX

O St. Joseph, whose protection is so great, so strong, so prompt before the throne of God, I place in you all my interest and desires. O St. Joseph, assist me by your powerful intercession, and obtain for me from your divine Son all spiritual blessings, through Jesus Christ, our Lord. So that, having engaged here below your heavenly power, I may offer my thanksgiving and homage to the most loving of fathers. O St. Joseph, I never weary contemplating you, and Jesus asleep in your arms; I dare not approach while He reposes near your heart. Press Him in my name, and kiss His fine head for me and ask Him to return the kiss when I draw my dying breath. St. Joseph, patron of departing souls, pray for me. Amen.

Remember, O most chaste spouse of the Virgin Mary, that never has it been known that anyone who asked for your help and sought your intercession was left unaided. Full of confidence in your power, I hasten to you, and beg your protection. Listen, O foster father of the Redeemer, to my humble prayer, and in your goodness hear and answer me. Amen.

The Blessed Sacrament and St. Joseph: Behold our help in these perilous times!

BISHOP PETER ANASTASIUS PICHENOT

NINE

"THE SUN OF THE FEASTS OF THE CHURCH"
Special Days and Seasons
Eucharistic Adoration Throughout the Year

I say that if our Lord were not living in His Sacrament, all our Christian feast days would be nothing but a series of funeral services. The Eucharist is the Sun of the feasts of the Church. It sheds light on those feasts and renders them living and joyous.

ST. PETER JULIAN EYMARD

This is the day which the Lord has made;
let us rejoice and be glad in it.
PSALM 118:24

For our paschal Lamb, Christ, has been sacrificed.
Therefore let us celebrate the feast.
1 CORINTHIANS 5:7-8, NAB

The Season of Advent

Jesus,... the Eucharist is the sacramental testimony of Your first coming, with which the words of the prophets were reconfirmed and expectations were fulfilled. You have left us, O Lord, Your Body and Blood under the species of bread and wine that they may bear witness to the fact that the world has been redeemed—that through them Your paschal mystery may reach all men as the Sacrament of life and salvation. The Eucharist is at the same time a constant announcement of Your second coming and the sign of the definitive Advent and also of the expectation of the whole Church.

When we eat this bread and drink this cup, we proclaim Your death, Lord Jesus, until You come in glory. Every day and every hour we wish to adore You, stripped under the species of bread and wine, to renew the hope of the call to glory... Amen.

POPE JOHN PAUL II

The Feast of the Nativity of Our Lord (Christmas)

The Word again becomes flesh and dwells among us, veiled under the species of the sacred Host, where the same Jesus born two thousand years ago as a little Babe in Bethlehem is truly, really, bodily, and personally present to us in this Most Blessed Sacrament.

MOTHER TERESA OF CALCUTTA

Raise Your tiny hand, divine Child,
and bless these young friends of Yours,
bless the children of all the earth.

POPE JOHN PAUL II

It is part of our Father's love that inside the pale of the Church earth should be one perpetual, and even ubiquitous, Bethlehem. The infant Jesus, the joy of the Father and our joy, is forever there, and in Him the Father declared, with rare expletive, that He was well pleased. Still on the altar and in the tabernacle the Babe of Bethlehem is increasing the glory of the Father.

FR. FREDERICK WILLIAM FABER

To Our Lady on Christmas Eve, Before the Blessed Sacrament
Mother of God,
Ark of the Covenant,
Tabernacle of the Lord,
Throne of the Most High,
Vessel of the Almighty,
Treasury of the Most Precious,
Home of the Most Holy!

Your sacred shadow falls
across this room,
where gold and crystal—
poor images of you at best—
hold your beloved Son
in sweet stillness.

In the silence
I hear you hum a lullaby
of adoration, comfort;
for where the Child is,
there too will be the Mother.

I have woven Him
a blanket of my praises:
ragged and rough,
soiled and smelling of earth.
Take it, my Lady,
and hem it round with your prayers,
wash it with your tears,
smooth it out with your graces,
sprinkle it with the fragrance
of your glory.

Only then will it be a fit covering
for my Lord,
the Son of Mary,
the Son of God.

PAUL THIGPEN

The Bethlehem of that night ... has never passed away. It lives a real life ... in the worshipful reality of the Blessed Sacrament. Round the tabernacle, which is our abiding Bethlehem, goes on the same world of beautiful devotion which surrounded the newborn Babe, real, out of real hearts, and realized by God's acceptance.

FR. FREDERICK WILLIAM FABER

The Season of Lent

I saw the Lord sitting upon a throne, high and lifted up.... And I said: "Woe is me! For I am lost; for I am a man of unclean lips, and I dwell in the midst of a people of unclean lips; for my eyes have seen the King, the Lord of hosts!"

ISAIAH 6:1, 5

Give me, good Lord, a full faith and a fervent charity, a love of You, good Lord, incomparably above the love of myself; and that I love nothing that displeases You but everything for the sake of You.

Take from me, good Lord, this lukewarm—or rather cold-hearted—way of meditation and this dullness in praying to You. And give me warmth, delight, and life in thinking of You. And give me grace to long for Your holy Sacraments, and specially to rejoice in the presence of Your blessed Body, sweet Savior Christ, in the holy Sacrament of the altar, and duly to thank You for Your precious visitation through it; and at that high Memorial, may I have grace to remember and consider Your most bitter passion with tender compassion.

St. Thomas More

The Feast of the Resurrection of Christ (Easter)

Holy Easter! The Lamb who was slain is the Lamb who is risen! Jesus in the Most Blessed Sacrament is the Lamb of God! Worthy is the Lamb! O come let us behold Him who has won for us salvation! O come let us adore Him, for the Bread of Life—Jesus Eucharistic—is really and personally here! May Jesus in the Most Blessed Sacrament, the Lamb of love, be with you and bless you this Easter and always! May our Lady of the Most Blessed Sacrament, Mother of the Lamb, lead you ever closer to His Eucharistic Heart!

Pope John Paul II

On Easter Night, Before the Blessed Sacrament
In Your round, white festal garment
I see the figures of a silent Paschal tale:
the morsel of betrayal,

the moon bathing garden agony,
the Roman pavement stone,
the sun ashamed to shine,
the napkin over folded eyes,
the tombstone flung away,
the evening Loaf of travelers
awakened to their Lord.

This is my Emmaus:
Stay with me, Lord,
for the day is far spent.
Come to my table
grant me Your blessing
open this dullard's eyes
for I would see You
in the Bread.

PAUL THIGPEN

The Feast of Pentecost

On my knees before the great multitude of heavenly witnesses, I offer myself soul and body to You, Eternal Spirit of God. I adore the brightness of Your purity, the unerring keenness of Your justice, and the might of Your love. You are the Strength and Light of my soul. In You I live and move and have my being. I desire never to grieve You by unfaithfulness to grace, and I pray with all my heart to be kept from the smallest sin against You.

Mercifully guard my every thought and grant that I may always watch for Your light and listen to Your voice and follow Your gracious inspirations. I cling to You and give myself to You and ask You by Your compassion to watch over me in my weakness. Holding the pierced feet of Jesus and looking at His five wounds and trusting in His precious Blood and adoring His opened side and stricken heart, I implore You, adorable Spirit, Helper of my infirmity, so to keep me in Your grace that I may never sin against You.

Give me grace, O Holy Spirit, Spirit of the Father and the Son, to say to You always and everywhere, *Speak Lord, for Your servant is listening.* Amen.

On Pentecost, Before the Blessed Sacrament
Eternal Holy Spirit,
blazing Oven of this Loaf
sweet Aroma of this Bread
Dove come down to turn this gift
into Godhead:
bake me in the furnace of Your heart
fill me with the fragrance of Your banquet
alight on me, abide in me
Spirit of Jesus
Come!

PAUL THIGPEN

The Feast of Corpus Christi

On Corpus Christi, Before the Blessed Sacrament
You languish in the darkness like
a criminal imprisoned
a sick man quarantined
an eccentric, babbling uncle, hid away.

Are they so afraid of You?
Are we so ashamed of You?
This is Your pageant day!

    Where are Your holy cavalcades?
    Your solemn ranks of soldiers
    with their Captain at their head?
    Your festal, fair processions
    winding through the curious crowds
    who marvel at the sacred spectacle?

In the quiet I hear echoes
from the stones of ancient streets
crying out with praise to shame us
for our silence.
In the blackness I see faces
of a multitude of children
looking down the ages, wondering
to see so plain a feast.

For the glory due Your name,
how long, O Lord,
must You wait?

PAUL THIGPEN

The Feast of the Sacred Heart of Jesus

O most sacred, most loving heart of Jesus, Thou art concealed in the Holy Eucharist, and Thou beatest for us still.... Thou art the heart of the Most High made man.... Thy Sacred Heart is the instrument and organ of Thy love. It did beat for us. It yearned for us. It ached for our salvation. It was on fire through zeal, that the glory of God might be manifest in and by us.... In worshipping thee I worship my incarnate God, my Emmanuel.

VENERABLE JOHN HENRY NEWMAN

Devotion to the Sacred Heart should bring us to a life of intimate union with Jesus who, we know, is truly present and living in the Eucharist. The two devotions, *to the Sacred Heart and to the Eucharist,* are closely connected. They call upon one another and, we may even say, they require one another. The Sacred Heart explains the mystery of the love of Jesus by which He becomes bread in order to nourish us with His substance, while in the Eucharist we have the real presence of this same Heart, living in our midst.

FR. GABRIEL OF ST. MARY MAGDALEN, O.C.D.

O Jesus, most sweet Jesus, hidden under the sacramental species, give me now such love and humility that I may be able lovingly to speak of this Invention of boundless love, that all who hear of it may begin to love You in reality.

O good Lord! O great Lord! How humbly You hide Yourself for our sake! But alas, how much are Your bounty and Your love abused! Not only do sinners despise You in this Sacrament of love, because they fail to see You, but even the good and the just treat You with indifference and coldness.

You have been with them so long, and they with You, that for lack of a lively faith they have not known You. Though You have been with us so long, there are only a few who know it, only a few who are penetrated with a sense of their unspeakable blessedness.

I hear You complain about us, O dear Jesus: "Behold this heart of Mine, so full of love for men that it has shed its last drop of Blood for them! I have given them My own Flesh and Blood as food and drink for their souls. Consider how this heart receives from most souls, in return for so great a love, nothing but ingratitude and contempt. But what grieves Me most is that I am thus treated even by good and just souls."

ST. MARGARET MARY ALACOQUE

To keep me from sin and straying from Him, God has used devotion to the Sacred Heart of Jesus in the Blessed Sacrament. My life vows are destined to be spent in the light irradiating from the tabernacle, and it is to the Heart of Jesus that I dare go for the solution of all my problems.

BLESSED POPE JOHN XXIII

The Feast of the Divine Mercy

You left us Yourself in the Sacrament of the altar, and You opened wide Your mercy to us. There is no misery that could exhaust You; You have called us all to this fountain of love, to this spring of God's compassion. Here is the Tabernacle of Your mercy, here is the remedy for all our ills. To You, O living Spring of mercy, all souls are drawn; some like deer, thirsting for Your love, others to wash the wound of their sins, and still others, exhausted by life, to draw strength.

O Jesus, concealed in the Blessed Sacrament of the altar, my only love and mercy, I commend to You all the needs of my body and soul. You can help me, because You are Mercy itself. In You lies all my hope. Be adored, O God, in the work of Your mercy, be blessed by all faithful hearts on whom Your gaze rests, in whom dwells Your immortal life.

ST. FAUSTINA KOWALSKA

Prayers of the Chaplet of Divine Mercy
Eternal Father, I offer You the Body and Blood, Soul and Divinity of Your dearly beloved Son, our Lord Jesus Christ, in atonement for our sins and those of the whole world.

For the sake of Your sorrowful passion, have mercy on us and on the whole world.

Holy God, Holy Mighty One, Holy Immortal One, have mercy on us and on the whole world.

The Feast of All Saints
Saints of God, perfected in love and victorious over sin, who now enjoy the reward of adoring Our Lord face to face in everlasting joy and glory: Be gracious to remember us, flawed and failing, who still struggle on earth, who kneel here adoring Our Lord hidden in the tabernacle, who long for the day when we too will be made like Him and will see Him as He is.

Gather around us here in His Eucharistic Presence to strengthen us with your prayers and to enrich our feeble worship with the mighty chorus of your praise. Teach us by your example to love Him above all things, so that we too may become the pure in heart who see God, who enjoy with you the eternal blessed fellowship of the Father, the Son, and the Holy Spirit. Amen.

The Feast of All Souls

Eternal Father, I offer You the most precious Blood of Your divine Son, Jesus, in union with the Masses said throughout the world today, for all the Holy Souls in purgatory. Amen.

St. Gertrude the Great

Help, Lord, the souls that Thou hast made, the souls
   to Thee so dear,
In prison for the debt unpaid of sin committed here.
These holy souls, they suffer on, resigned in heart and will,
Until Thy high behest is done, and justice has its fill.
For daily falls, for pardoned crime, they joy to undergo
The shadow of Thy cross sublime, the remnant of Thy woe.
Oh, by their patience of delay, their hope amid their pain,
Their sacred zeal to burn away disfigurement and stain;
Oh, by their fire of love, not less in keenness
   than the flame;
Oh, by their very helplessness, Oh, by Thine own great name,
Good Jesus, help! Sweet Jesus, aid the souls to Thee most dear
In prison for the debt unpaid of sins committed here.

Venerable John Henry Newman

Receive, Lord, in tranquility and peace, the souls of Your servants who have departed out of this present life to be with You. Give them the life that knows no age, the good things that do not pass away; through Jesus Christ our Lord. Amen.

ST. IGNATIUS LOYOLA

Feast of Christ the King

Almighty and merciful God, You break the power of evil and make all things new in Your Son Jesus Christ, the King of the universe. May all in heaven and earth acclaim Your glory and never cease to praise You.

We ask this through our Lord Jesus Christ, Your Son, who lives and reigns with You and the Holy Spirit, one God, forever and ever. Amen.

Crown Him with many crowns, the Lamb upon His throne.
Hark! how the heavenly anthem drowns all music but its own.
Awake, my soul, and sing of Him who died for thee,
and hail Him as thy matchless King through all eternity.

Crown Him the Lord of love! Behold His hands and side,
those wounds, yet visible above, in beauty glorified;
No angel in the sky can fully bear that sight,
but downward bend His wondering eye at mysteries so bright.

Crown Him the Lord of years! The potentate of time,
Creator of the rolling spheres, ineffably sublime!
All hail, Redeemer, hail! For Thou hast died for me;
Thy praise shall never, never fail throughout eternity.

MATTHEW BRIDGES

TEN

"THE RADICAL TRANSFORMATION OF THE WORLD"
Mission
The Power and Promise of Eucharistic Adoration

Closeness to Christ in silence and contemplation does not distance us from our contemporaries but, on the contrary, makes us attentive and open to human joy and distress and broadens our heart on a global scale. It unites us with our brothers and sisters in humanity.... Through adoration, the Christian mysteriously contributes to the radical transformation of the world and to the sowing of the Gospel.

POPE JOHN PAUL II

It is that Sacrament, and that alone, the Christ living in our midst, and sacrificed by us, and for us and with us, in the clean and perpetual Sacrifice, it is He alone who holds our world together, and keeps us all from being poured headlong and immediately into the pit of our eternal destruction. And I tell you there is a power that goes forth from that Sacrament, a power of light and truth, even into the hearts of those who have heard nothing of Him and seem to be incapable of belief.

THOMAS MERTON

O blessed Host, our only hope in the midst of the darkness and godlessness that inundate the earth!

St. Faustina Kowalska

Anyone who prays to the Savior draws the whole world with him and raises it to God. Those who stand before the Lord are therefore fulfilling an eminent service. They are presenting to Christ all those who do not know Him or are far from Him; they keep watch in His presence on their behalf.

Pope John Paul II

A Prayer of Hope, Before the Blessed Sacrament

Within Your small circumference,
my Eucharistic Lord,
I see the world entire,
an image of the globe as You made it:
pure round planet
lovingly crafted,
playfully spinning,
laden with hope and promise.

Within Your shadow,
my Eucharistic Lord,
I see the world as well,
an image of the world as it became:
dark round abyss
hollowed out in rebellion,
yawning in malice,
swirling with rage and despair.

But into the maw
of that black hole of sin
You have tossed this tiny Orb
of Your divinity.
The blackness swallows
but chokes:
Death must die.

   For this humble Star has burst
   into a glorious Supernova
   filling the abyss,
   slaying the darkness,
   transfiguring the heavens
   with the splendor of a billion suns.

Draw me in,
my Eucharistic Lord,
by Your gravity of goodness;
set ablaze, set me spinning
into orbit around You.
Lead me in Your radiant train,
a bright speck
in Your galaxy of grace.

PAUL THIGPEN

I do not cease to give thanks for you, remembering you in my prayers, that the God of our Lord Jesus Christ, the Father of glory, may give you a spirit of wisdom and of revelation in the knowledge of him, having the eyes of your hearts enlightened, that you may know what is the hope to which he has called you, what are the riches of his glorious inheritance in the saints, and what is the immeasurable greatness of his power in us who believe.

EPHESIANS 1:16-19

It was not until ... we began our daily Holy Hour that our community started to grow and blossom.... We have much work to do. Our homes for the sick and dying destitute are full everywhere. And from the time we started having adoration every day, our love for Jesus became more intimate, our love for each other more understanding, our love for the poor more compassionate, and we have double the number of vocations. God has blessed us with many wonderful vocations. The time we spend in having our daily audience with God is the most precious part of the whole day.

MOTHER TERESA OF CALCUTTA

Lord Jesus, who in the Eucharist make Your dwelling among us and become our traveling companion, sustain our Christian communities so that they may be ever more open to listening and accepting Your Word. May they draw from the Eucharist a renewed commitment to spreading in society, by the proclamation of Your gospel, the signs and deeds of an attentive and active charity.

POPE JOHN PAUL II

The Blessed Sacrament is indeed the stimulus for us all, for me as it should be for you, to forsake all worldly ambitions. Without the constant presence of our Divine Master upon the altar in my poor chapels, I never could have persevered casting my lot with the lepers of Molokai.

BLESSED JOSEPH DE VEUSTER (FR. DAMIEN)

He draws us to Himself by grace, by example, by power, by lovingness, by beauty, by pardon, and above all by the Blessed Sacrament. Everyone who has had anything to do with ministering to souls has seen the power which Jesus has. Talent is not needed. Eloquence is comparatively unattractive. Learning is often beside the mark. Controversy simply repels.... All the attraction of the Church is in Jesus, and His chief attraction is the Blessed Sacrament.

FR. FREDERICK WILLIAM FABER

It took me a long time as a convert to realize the presence of Christ as Man in the Sacrament.... He is our Leader who is always with us. Do you wonder that Catholics are exultant in the knowledge that their Leader is with them?

DOROTHY DAY

In the Eucharist we behold as in a mirror what we shall be enabled to contemplate face to face in eternity. We thus can face up to the burden of living filled with the strength of the Eucharist and the hope of rising again. This hope also confers special characteristics on human freedom. It teaches patience, perseverance, self-giving, and sacrifice. And it shows us that the risen Christ is the source and measure of the fullness of freedom.

Pontifical Committee for International Eucharistic Congresses

Eucharistic heart of Jesus,
Furnace of divine love,
set the world afire!

O my divine Lord in the Blessed Sacrament, I offer You my body and its senses, my soul and its faculties, my heart and its sentiments. My thoughts, my desires, my words, my actions, my whole being are Yours. Since You have given Yourself wholly to me, can I do less than give myself wholly to You? Grant me, O divine Jesus, to persevere in Your holy love. Give me a still greater sorrow for my past sins, and strengthen the sincere resolution I have formed never again to offend You. Amen.

The thought of the presence of God and the spirit of worship will in all my actions have as their immediate object Jesus, God and Man, really present in the most holy Eucharist. The spirit of sacrifice, of humiliation, of scorn for self in the eyes of men, will be illuminated, supported, and strengthened by the constant thought of Jesus, humiliated and despised in the Blessed Sacrament.

Blessed Pope John XXIII

Eucharistic worship is not so much worship of the inaccessible transcendence as worship of the divine condescension; and it is the merciful and redeeming transformation of the world in the human heart.

POPE JOHN PAUL II

O sweet Sacrament of Love! we belong to Thee, for Thou art our living Love Himself. Thou art our well of life, for in Thee is the divine Life Himself, immeasurable, compassionate, eternal.... There shall not be a single thought, a single hope, a single wish, which shall not be all for Thee!

FR. FREDERICK WILLIAM FABER

Adoration will heal our Church and thus our nation and thus our world.... When we adore, we plug into infinite dynamism and power. Adoration is more powerful for construction than nuclear bombs are for destruction.

PETER KREEFT

Where cross the crowded ways of life, where sound the cries
    of race and clan,
above the noise of selfish strife we hear Thy voice,
    O Son of Man!
In haunts of wretchedness and need, on shadowed thresholds
    dark with fears,
from paths where hide the lures of greed, we catch the vision
    of Thy tears.

From tender childhood's helplessness, from woman's grief,
   man's burdened toil,
from famished souls, from sorrowed stress, Thy heart has
   never known recoil.
The cup of water given for Thee still holds the freshness
   of Thy grace;
yet long these multitudes to see the sweet compassion
   of Thy face.
O Master from the mountainside, make haste to heal these
   hearts of pain;
among these restless throngs abide. Oh, tread
   the city's streets again!

FRANK MASON NORTH

I know I would not be able to work one week if it were not for that continual force coming from Jesus in the Blessed Sacrament.

MOTHER TERESA OF CALCUTTA

Our own belief is that the renovation of the world will be brought about only by the Holy Eucharist.

POPE LEO XIII

I carry Your image, O Sacred Host, engraved in my memory, but far more in my heart; my looks and my thoughts, piercing brick walls, silk, the precious metals, and even the appearance of bread which hides You, my Jesus.

SERVANT OF GOD CONCEPCIÓN CABRERA DE ARMIDA

As God draws near, He takes on the form of bread and wine in the Eucharist. He has become food for our souls.... Through this way of the Sacrament of the Eucharist, He has overcome every limit that man could ever imagine.

POPE JOHN PAUL II

When the Sisters are exhausted, up to their eyes in work; when all seems to go awry, they spend an hour in prayer before the Blessed Sacrament. This practice has never failed to bear fruit: They experience peace and strength.

MOTHER TERESA OF CALCUTTA

As this visit of adoration closes, O Jesus, I renew my faith and trust in You. I am refreshed after these moments with You, and I count myself among a privileged number, even as Your disciples were, who shared Your actual presence.

Realizing that my visit to You is of little avail unless I try to live a better life and set a better example, I am resolved to go forth again to my duties and my concerns with a renewed spirit of perseverance and good will. In my daily life I will try to love and serve God well, and love my neighbor also, for these two things go together. I will try to be a true disciple, indeed. Help me, O Jesus, in this my resolution.

CARDINAL JOHN J. CARBERRY

Eucharistic worship constitutes the soul of all Christian life. In fact, Christian life is expressed in the fulfilling of the greatest commandment, that is to say, in the love of God and neighbor, and this love finds its source in the Blessed Sacrament, which is commonly called the Sacrament of love.... A living fruit of this worship is the perfecting of the image of God that we bear within us.

POPE JOHN PAUL II

We must live our commitment to society
steeped in the Eucharist.

ARCHBISHOP NICOLAS COTUGNO

My Jesus, I must leave You now, but I will yearn to return. May I love You ever present in the Eucharist—ever treasure the holy sacrifice of the Mass, receive You devoutly in Holy Communion, and adore You present in the Most Blessed Sacrament.... May my heart be a lamp the light of which shall burn and beam for You. Amen.

CARDINAL JOHN J. CARBERRY

The Eucharist strikes such fire within us that we are compelled by our actions and our presence to warm the people we live among and to melt the ice of hate, discrimination, indifference, injustice, and isolation. "Can a man hide fire in his bosom and his garments not burn?" (Proverbs 6:27).

FR. FRANKLYN M. MCAFEE

Before Leaving the Presence of the Blessed Sacrament

Food of the world,
how long before the world
comes to Your table?
Banquet of love,
highways, byways,
teem with starving souls
not yet aware
that empty chairs await them.
How can I compel them
to come in?

Make me this day
the envelope of Your invitation,
the aroma of Your feast,
the song of Your minstrel,
the banner on Your door.
Let every movement of my days announce:
Come feed on the Bread of life!

PAUL THIGPEN

O Jesus, present in the Sacrament of the altar, teach all the nations to serve You with willing hearts, knowing that to serve God is to reign. May Your Sacrament, O Jesus, be light to the mind, strength to the will, joy to the heart. May it be the support of the weak, the comfort of the suffering, the wayfaring bread of salvation for the dying, and for all, the promise of future glory.

BLESSED POPE JOHN XXIII

And Jesus came and said to them, "All authority in heaven and on earth has been given to Me. Go therefore and make disciples of all nations, baptizing them in the name of the Father and of the Son and of the Holy Spirit, teaching them to observe all that I have commanded you; and lo, I am with you always, to the close of the age."

MATTHEW 28:18-20

Index

Sources and Further Reading

à Kempis, Thomas. *The Imitation of Christ.*

Ancient Devotions for Holy Communion. Ft. Collins, Colo.: Roman Catholic Books (reprint), n.d.

Augustine of Hippo. *Restless Till We Rest in You: 60 Reflections from the Writings of St. Augustine.* Edited by Paul Thigpen. Ann Arbor, Mich.: Servant, 1998.

The Blessed Sacrament: God With Us. Rockford, Ill.: TAN, n.d.

Buckley, Michael. *The Catholic Prayer Book.* Edited by Tony Castle. Ann Arbor, Mich.: Servant, 1986.

Carberry, John J. *Reflections and Prayers for Visits With Our Eucharistic Lord.* Boston: Pauline, 1992.

Catechism of the Catholic Church. Liguori, Mo.: Liguori, 1994.

de Armida, Concepción Cabrera. *Before the Altar.* Translated by Luisa Icaza de Medina Mora. Mexico: Ediciones Cimiento, A.C., 1913, 1988.

de Sales, Francis. *Introduction to the Devout Life.* Rockford, Ill.: TAN, 1994.

Dollen, Charles J., ed. *Traditional Catholic Prayers.* Huntington, Ind.: Our Sunday Visitor, 1990.

Eymard, Peter Julian. *The Eymard Library,* vols. 1-9. Cleveland: Congregation of the Blessed Sacrament, 1947.

——. *My Eucharistic Day: Rules and Practices Recommended by St. Peter Julian Eymard.* Libertyville, Ill.: Franciscan Marytown Press, 1954.

Faber, Frederick William. *The Blessed Sacrament.* Rockford, Ill.: TAN, 1978.

Groeschel, Benedict J., and James Monti. *In the Presence of Our Lord: The History, Theology and Psychology of Eucharistic Devotion.* Huntington, Ind.: Our Sunday Visitor, 1997.

Guernsey, Daniel P., ed. *Adoration: Eucharistic Texts and Prayers*

Throughout Church History. San Francisco: Ignatius, 1999.

Hardon, John A. *Catechism on the Real Presence.* Bardstown, Ky.: Eternal Life, 1998.

Pope John Paul II. *Celebrate 2000! Reflections on Jesus, the Holy Spirit and the Father.* Edited by Paul Thigpen. Ann Arbor, Mich.: Servant, 1996.

——. *Dominicae Cenae.*

——. *The Prayers of Pope John Paul II.* Edited by Paul Thigpen. Ann Arbor, Mich.: Servant, 1996.

——. *Redemptor Hominis.*

Korn, Daniel. *Prayers and Devotions for Eucharistic Holy Hour.* Liguori, Mo.: Liguori, 2000.

Kowalska, Faustina. *Divine Mercy in My Soul: The Diary of Servant of God Sr. M. Faustina Kowalska.* Stockbridge, Mass.: Marian, 1987.

Liguori, Alphonsus. *The Holy Eucharist.* Edited by Charles Dollen. New York: Alba, 1994.

——. *Visits to the Most Blessed Sacrament and the Blessed Virgin Mary.* Rockford, Ill.: TAN, n.d.

Lovasik, Lawrence G. *Treasury of Novenas.* New York: Catholic Book Publishing, 1986.

Manelli, Stefano M. *Jesus Our Eucharistic Love: Eucharistic Life Exemplified by the Saints.* New Bedford, Mass.: Franciscan Friars of the Immaculate, 1996.

The Manual of Catholic Prayer: For All Days and Seasons and Every Circumstance of Christian Life. New York: Harper & Row, 1961.

McHugh, Joan Carter, ed. *My Daily Eucharist.* Lake Forest, Ill.: Witness Ministries, 1995.

——. *My Daily Eucharist II.* Lake Forest, Ill.: Witness Ministries, 1997.

Menendez, Josefa. *The Way of Divine Love.* Enfield, England: Sands, 1949.

Merton, Thomas. *The Seven Story Mountain.* Garden City, NY: Image, 1970.

More, Thomas. *Be Merry in God: 60 Reflections from the Writings of St. Thomas More.* Edited by Paul Thigpen. Ann Arbor, Mich.: Servant, 1999.

Mueller, Michael. *The Blessed Eucharist.* Baltimore: Kelley & Piet, 1868.

Pope Paul VI. *Mysterium Fidei.*

Ramirez, Josefino S., and Vincent Martin Lucia. *Letters to a Brother Priest.* Plattsburgh, N.Y.: Missionaries of the Blessed Sacrament, 1998.

Reuter, Frederick A. *Moments Divine Before the Blessed Sacrament: Historic and Legendary Readings and Prayers.* New York: H.L. Kilner, 1922.

Socias, James, ed. *Handbook of Prayers.* Princeton, N.J.: Sceptre/Chicago:Midwest Theological Forum, 1998.

Thérèse of Lisieux. *Poems of Sr. Teresa.* Translated by S.L. Emery. Boston: Angel Guardian Press, 1907.

Trevino, José Guadalupe. *The Holy Eucharist.* Milwaukee: Brucc, 1947.